CREATING WEALTH

The Art of Investing In Real Estate

Benjamin Oyortey Sr.

Creating Wealth: The Art of Investing In Real Estate

www.realestateinvestmentwealth.com

Copyright © 2018 Benjamin Oyortey

ISBN-13: 978-1727055184
ISBN-10: 1727055187

All rights reserved. No portion of this book may be reproduced mechanically, electronically, or by any other means, including photocopying, without permission of the publisher or author except in the case of brief quotations embodied in critical articles and reviews. It is illegal to copy this book, post it to a website, or distribute it by any other means without permission from the publisher or author.

Limits of Liability and Disclaimer of Warranty
The author and publisher shall not be liable for your misuse of the enclosed material. This book is strictly for informational and educational purposes only.

Warning – Disclaimer
The purpose of this book is to educate and entertain. The author and/or publisher do not guarantee that anyone following these techniques, suggestions, tips, ideas, or strategies will become successful. The author and/or publisher shall have neither liability nor responsibility to anyone with respect to any loss or damage caused, or alleged to be caused, directly or indirectly by the information contained in this book.

Publisher
10-10-10 Publishing
Markham, ON
Canada

Printed in Canada and the United States of America

CONTENTS

Dedication	ix
Foreword	xi
Acknowledgements	xiii

CHAPTER 1: Why Real Estate 1
Why I Am In Real Estate	1
Your Why	4
The Real Meaning Of Wealth	5
Differentiate Yourself	7
Have A Clear Vision	7
Attitude Matters	8
Aim High	9
The Power Of Focus	10
Be Prepared: Study, Study, Study	14
Believe In Yourself And Don't Give Up	15

CHAPTER 2: Effective Strategies For Dealing With Clients 21
The Customer Matters	21
Listening To The Customer	23
Provide Quality Work and Exceed Expectations	25
Landlording	28
Hire Your Own Cleaning Crew	32
Hire a Hauling Company	32

Dealing with The Seller 34
Hiring A Sales Person 34
Dealing with the Buyer 35
Exceed Your Clients' Expectations 36
Communication 38
Avoid Creating Unhappy Clients 38

Chapter 3: Proven Ways To Find Deals 41
Real Estate Agent 41
Marketing 46
Direct Mail 47
Probate/Inherited Properties 49
Divorce Attorneys 50
Yellow Letter 51
Expired Listings 53
Federal Express Envelope 54
Lumpy Mail 55
Postcard 55
Invitation Envelope 56
Internet 56
Social Media 57
Bird Dogs 57
Bandit signs 58
Classified Ads 61
Auctions 62

Chapter 4: Proven Ways To Analyze Deals 65
Repairs 68
Other Costs 69

Formulas to Consider When Evaluating Deals	70
Other Considerations Before You Buy	78
Wholesaling	79
Lease Option	83

Chapter 5: Proven Ways to Negotiate and Buy Properties — 85

When to Buy and When to Walk Away	85
Know What the Other Side is Looking For	89
Do Your Due Diligence	89
Meeting With Your Real Estate Agent	90
The Research Phase	91
Be Careful About What You Say	92
The Pregnant Pause Technique	94
Do Not Be Lazy	95
Listening To The Seller Is Key	96
Make Her Feel Good	97
Ask For Concessions	99
Keep Your Excitement To Minimum	101
Presenting Low Offers	102
Ask Questions	102
Drop Your Pride	104
Be Willing to Compromise	105

Chapter 6: Proven Ways to Acquire Properties — 107

Strategy 1. Lease With An Option To Purchase	108
Strategy 2: Short Sales	117
Strategy 3: Expired Listings	122
Strategy 4: Subject To	123
Strategy 5: Wholesaling	126

Chapter 7: Proven Ways to Increase the Value of Your Property — **129**

The External	132
Landscaping	133
Trees	134
Garage/Carport	135
Power Washing	135
The Inside	137
Paint the House	137
Great Room/Living Room	138
Bedroom	139
Bathroom	141
Kitchen	145
Basement	147

Chapter 8: Proven Ways To Raise Money To Fund Deals — **151**

Financial Institutions	152
Hard Money Loans	154
Credit Cards	157
Partnerships	158
Private Funds	160
Direct Mailing	164

Chapter 9: Best Ways to Market and Sell Your Properties (Part 1) — **169**

Real Estate Agent	169
For Sale By Owner (FSBO)	176
Final Word	184

Chapter 10: Best Ways to Market and Sell Your Properties (Part 2) — 185

- Photographs — 185
- Virtual Tours — 188
- Classified Ads — 189
- Flyers — 191
- Post Cards — 193
- Direct Mailing — 193
- Social Media — 194
- Open Houses — 195
- Good Marketing Tips — 196
- Avoid Bad Marketing — 197

Chapter 11: Get A Power Team Together — 203

- Real Estate Agent — 207
- Appraiser — 208
- Contractor — 210
- Accountant — 214
- Insurance Agent — 215
- Mortgage Broker — 217
- Private-Money Lenders — 217
- Attorney — 218

About the Author — 219

*This book is dedicated to my family:
my loving wife, Michele;
my amazing and incredible sons,
Benjamin Nartey Jr., Joshua Kwame,
and Josiah Mensah.*

FOREWORD

Before you think about investing in real estate, I would highly recommend that you read this book in its entirety.

Although several books have been written on creating wealth, and on real estate investing, *Creating Wealth* is the first book I've read that combines the two concepts, and gives a step-by-step approach to how to become wealthy through the art of investing in real estate. Benjamin Oyortey has really taken the time to nail this concept in his book.

As rightly stated, real estate investing is indeed an art that must be learned. That is why this book is a must-read. If you do not know what you are getting yourself into, you may end up wasting a lot of precious time and money, chasing after the wind just trying to understand and reinvent the wheel of wealth creation through the process of real estate investing. I call that a disaster that you want to avoid.

One of the fascinating things about this book is the passion and in-depth knowledge that Benjamin has mastered and included in its pages. He did not only state facts but has given practical examples of how he started. He chronicled the odds that he had to face, which makes him an expert on the subject matter. Who better to learn from than from the one that has already seen the good, the bad and the ugly in real estate investing and wealth creation?

This book takes you from your *Why*, to the ways that you can find deals. It also teaches you how you can effortlessly generate funds to close on your deals quickly, without borrowing from the banks.

Benjamin is a master entrepreneur who has worked, and continues to work, with many clients, including fund managers, real estate agents, investors and homeowners. Benjamin teaches you through the masterpiece of *Creating Wealth: The Art of Investing In Real Estate* about how not to do the work alone but with what he calls a "Dream Team."

I applaud the tremendous amount of time and the wealth of knowledge that Benjamin has placed in his book. He will help you master the art of investing and propel you to start creating the wealth of your dreams.

Raymond Aaron
New York Bestselling Author

ACKNOWLEDGEMENTS

First and foremost, I would like to thank my Heavenly Father, who loves me dearly despite myself. He is the Lord of my life, without whom I am forever worthless. He has been there for me and has promised to continue to be with me through the vicissitudes of life.

I would like to thank you, my dear wife, **Michele**, my three strong boys, **Benjamin Jr.**, **Joshua Kwame, Josiah Mensah,** my brother and his lovely wife, **Samuel and Velda Oyortey,** and my mother-in-law, **Marie Vieux-Fort,** for your support and the space that you afforded me to write this book. I owe you a tremendous amount of gratitude.

I would like to acknowledge my parents of blessed memory, Ebenezer and Elizabeth Oyortey. The wisdom, knowledge, and understanding that they imparted to me is forever chronicled in my heart. Their toils and tears, the fear of God that they instilled in me as soon as I landed on planet earth, and their unconditional love, which knew no boundaries, are the reasons that I am here today, to impart the same gift that they shared with me to the rest of the world.

Dr. Jacob J. Nortey, only God knows how deeply I love and appreciate you. You have been a father and a role model to me. Through my ups and downs, through my academic years, from high school to graduate school and professional life, you have been there for me every step of the way. You have taught me how to be faithful in the little things in life. I owe you enormously and thank you. **Mrs. Thelma Nortey**, thank you for teaching me the intricacies of life. Your love, your relentless belief in me, and your care and instructions are forever chiseled in my heart.

What can I say about **Raymond Aaron**? He believed in me and pushed me and told me that I could I write a book on real estate. As my mentor, editor, and publisher, I owe you an immense gratitude. Your race to the North Pole was my inspiration. I convinced myself that if Raymond could race to the North Pole and win, then I could definitely write a book. I can now look back and say that I did it.

I would like to thank **Ron Legrand**, whose inspiration and conviction made me go into real estate with hope and determination. **Scott Scheel,** whose savviness in commercial real estate made me to want to learn more daily and think of the impossible. **Cameron Dunlap**, you said that if you could do it, then I could do it also. Thank you for allowing me to be part of your inner-circle. **Alan Cowgill**, you have taught and pushed me. Your passion and your willingness to allow me to sit with you and ask questions gave me the hope to raise as much money as I could to close on several deals. I owe you. Thank you.

Acknowledgements

Dr. Nido Quebin, I thank you for imparting enormous wisdom unto me through my mentor, who would never finish a conference session without mentioning your name. **Les Brown,** what an honor to finally meet you. Your words of wisdom and the passion that you bring to the speaking industry has been my motivation. No week passes by that I do not glean from your wisdom. I want to thank **Dr. John Grey**. You are funny, and full of life and inspiration. Your brilliance and great sense of humor is incredible. You light up a room with your presence. Thank you for the guidance that you gave me when I met you at a conference.

I would like to thank **Vena Cox** for her passion in real estate. Despite your busy schedule, you always took time to sit with me, and you not only answer my questions but provided guidance and the reason why I should walk away from certain deals that I thought made sense. Your teaching spirit, your patience, and the care that you bring to the real estate industry is extraordinary.

I am extremely grateful to you, **Connie Regan Green**. You are one of the most remarkable people that I have met. I appreciate your willingness to take me by the hand and teach me. You are genuine and authentic, and a caring mentor.

Lisa Nichols, what can I say about you? You are real, daring, audacious, loving, caring, and transparent. I am glad that you have taken me under your wing, not only as my mentor but as a sister. I love you, and I thank you for your willingness and assurance to always be there for me no matter what.

I would like to acknowledge and thank my friends: **Dr. Seth Laryea**, former president of Valley View University, and **Mrs. Uriel Laryea**, you have been a brother and a sister to me since my childhood years. **Geo-Stevens Aidoo** Esquire, head consultant, Advent Chambers: your drive and passion for education is unparalleled. You continue to push me to climb higher.

I also want to express my gratitude to **Earl Harris Sr.**, **Cynthia Harris**, **Mr. and Mrs. Troy Page Sr.**, **Dr. Elethia Dean**, **Dr. Shirley Benton**, **Sue Sugar**, **Ana Sosa**, **Dr. and Mrs. Charles Lokko**, **Shelly Corpman**, **Dr. Rachel Williams**, **Huria Kiran**, **Israel and Nipress Ndengabaganizi**, for being such astounding people. You have inspired me over the years, and you continue to support and cheer me on every day. You are truly incredible, and I am fortunate to have you in my life.

I want to express my gratitude to **James Lee, Robert Roesch, Barb Powers**, my book architect and **Lisa Browning**, my book editor. You have stood by me through many trials and tribulations. What a joy it is to call you my true partners.

Mr. Godwin Nxumalo and **Dr. Nozipho Nxumalo**, you are truly remarkable. Your energy and determination has rubbed off on me. Your sense of humor, and your love for my entire family is greatly appreciated. My boys truly regard you as their

Acknowledgements

grandparents, and I am thankful for you being there for us. You are forever part of our family.

The days that I get stiff due to long hours of sitting and writing, I am able to unwind by utilizing the facilities at LA Fitness and Metro Fitness, where **Mike Davis** was gracious enough to grant me membership, so I could reap the benefits of excising. It is because of the environment that you have created that I was able to remain sane after training and exercising my muscles. My training partners, **Eric** and **Darin**, made sure that I did not under or over exercise on days that I was so frustrated with myself. I am really honored. It is because of your friendship that I am able to write this book.

To **Troy Marsh** of Keller Williams Realty, thank you for taking it upon yourself to construct real estate deals that brought joy to my heart. To **Gloria Henry**, you have been with me for over eleven years as one of the best real estate agents that I could count on. You have represented me in various capacities, and I am highly appreciative of the knowledge that you bring to the real estate world.

Trevor Noah, your fearless spirit, your great sense of humor, your transparency and truthfulness kept me going during the days that I did not feel like writing. You are relentless and driven. These qualities kept me going anytime I tuned in to watch your show on Comedy Central. Thank you, brother.

CHAPTER 1

WHY REAL ESTATE

WHY I AM IN REAL ESTATE

"Some men see things as they are, and ask why. I dream of things that never were, and ask why not."
– Robert Kennedy

It was a beautiful and a gorgeous day as the Dean of the Graduate School of Business called my name to award me with a Master of Business Administration Degree. The applause, the screams of joy, the happiness written on the faces of all those who came to be with me and witness my graduation, was extraordinary. The Dean, the faculty, and my graduating class were all proud of me as I walked tall and stately, with a sense of accomplishment, to receive my MBA.

A day after my graduation, as I went back to campus to tie up some loose ends, I was greeted by my Corporate Finance and Short-term Finance professor, whom I will refer to as Dr. X. He began the conversation by congratulating me, and indicated how proud he felt as I received my degree on the previous day. Although he knew that I had already received several job offers from reputable companies, he wanted to know which company I was going to work for.

After I disclosed to him as to which company I decided to work for, he said something that has stayed with me to this day. "Congratulations, Ben; go and represent your school very well. Be sure to make lots of money for your company." I then thanked him for all his help, counseling, and teachings that groomed and prepared me for the corporate world.

It wasn't long after our conversation that the words, *"Be sure to make lots of money for your company,"* came back to haunt me. I started asking myself what that meant. Is this why I sacrificed everything to pursue my MBA? Where was I, Benjamin Oyortey, in the conversation with this finance tycoon, who just bought a house for over a million dollars, and is a well-accomplished professor, as well as a consultant for Fortune 500 companies?

How about me? I began to wrestle with myself, and wondered why I did not question him about his statement to me. Why did he not say, "Ben, be sure to do well, work hard, and make lots of money, and become wealthy and live in abundance so you can be of great value and asset to your family and humanity. Be sure to impact and transform millions of lives?" Why was he concerned about me making money for a company rather than creating wealth and abundance for my family and myself?

For a little over twelve years, I worked hard for one of the largest financial institutions in corporate America. I traveled extensively for my company. I worked long and tedious hours for my company. I trained managers for my company. I educated and mentored recent graduates with MBAs for my company. I was instrumental in recruiting excellent talents for my company.

However, despite all my efforts and accomplishments, I woke up one morning and realized that although I have my own house and possess a beautiful car, I was nowhere close to becoming wealthy. I was just like any other employee that did not own his time, and had to be dictated to as to when to take vacations, attend my children's special days, etc. I remember how I had to miss my own son's birthday to teach my BOSS and help him to finish a report, so he could look good in the eyes of senior management. I was just a number, an employee who lived from paycheck to paycheck. I was that employee who sometimes went home at midnight. I was that employee who on many occasions missed the evening meal with my family. I was that employee who did everything that I could to make my boss look good.

No matter how appreciative my manager was, the only pay raise that I received annually was between 3% and 4%. Is this what my business school professor meant when he encouraged me to make money for my company? And yes, he was right. I made plenty of money for my company but none for myself. It was at this point that I decided to hang up my corporate jersey, branch out into the world of entrepreneurship to create more value for the marketplace, and be paid handsomely for it. Once I made that decision, I left the well-paying JOB (Just Over Broke) behind to embark on creating wealth for myself and my family, rather than for a company. Although there are several industries that I could have gone into as I started on my journey to create wealth, I decided that real estate was the vehicle that would lead me on this journey.

YOUR WHY

Your WHY is the reason you do what you do. To become a real estate investor, you must have a firm idea as to why you want to become a real estate investor. To become wealthy, you must have a strong reason as to why you want to become wealthy. To do anything, there must be a robust, convincing reason why you want to do that thing. It is essential, therefore, that you define your WHY.

To give you an example, one of my two brothers died at a very young age, and left his wife and four children behind. I felt so obligated to help these children through high school, college, and graduate school. For me not to be in the position to help my nieces and nephews would be a colossal failure on my part. I, therefore, decided immediately that I would get up and find a way to become wealthy, turn around, and pull them along. I realized that the corporate 8 to 5 daily routine, which gave me two paychecks in a given month, would not help me to become wealthy. This got me on a path to research that one industry that could propel me to become wealthy. I analyzed different businesses, such as internet marketing, the stock market, and real estate. I then decided that the fastest way to achieve my goal was to become a real estate investor. This is my *why* for becoming a real estate investor.

How about you? At this point, I will ask you to stop reading. Take a notebook and write down *your why*. What is your REAL reason why you want to become a real estate investor? Your WHY must be HUGE, and it must be STRONG. It must be CONVINCING and it must be SPECIFIC; and it must be quantifiable and it must have a true COMPELLING MEANING for you. Once you complete this exercise, hang it on your bedroom wall, your office, or wherever you prefer, where you can see it daily. It must be cemented and concretized in your brain and psyche, and you must live it every day.

THE REAL MEANING OF WEALTH

What is wealth, you may ask? To become wealthy, you must understand what wealth means. Although there are several schools of thought as to what wealth means, I will look at wealth from a different point of view. Wealth, to me, is the abundance of valuable possessions or resources that you possess, coupled with the time, freedom, and flexibility to enjoy it.

One of the most valuable things that I learned in my finance class, Finance 101, is that Net Worth equals Assets minus Liabilities. Although this is a clear-cut definition, I will add that wealth is more than just bringing home paychecks from three different jobs. You could bring a handsome amount of money home each month. However, that does not constitute wealth.

According to our definition, once you receive your paycheck, you must subtract all your expenses from it (i.e., mortgage payment, utilities, groceries, dental expenses, medical expenses, lawn care, etc.). Then, you must also be sure to apply the freedom to enjoy what is left with your beloved family. So, with that said, let us analyze how you acquired the paychecks in the first place. In simple terms, you worked at three different locations or jobs, after which someone gave you three different paychecks.

This is what I call the VICIOUS CYCLE OF ENDING YOUR LIFE on earth VERY FAST. This, to me, is not wealth creation. Even if you have plenty of money left over, the mere fact that you are wasting your life away by working three different jobs, and not having enough time for yourself and your family, tells me that you do not have the flexibility or the freedom to enjoy the excess of your hard-earned money after all the bills are paid. With that said, let us look at my definition one more time. The word that I want you to emphasize is FREEDOM. You can work three different jobs and bring in a considerable amount of money, but without the FREEDOM to enjoy it with your family, you are not wealthy.

To be classified as a wealthy person, you must add all the assets that you own or possess, whether it is tangible or intangible. You must then subtract all the debts that you owe, from your income, and then add the flexibility or freedom to enjoy it. No one should have the audacity to dictate to you as to when to go on vacation with your family. No one should *approve* when you can be at your child's birthday or graduation. No one should *approve* when you deserve to take a leave of absence. Once you can do all the activities as mentioned above, plus more, without seeking permission from a BOSS or a SUPERVISOR, then you and I can agree that indeed, you are WEALTHY!

DIFFERENTIATE YOURSELF

Before you embark on the journey to financial freedom and wealth creation, there are several things that you must seriously consider. Some of the items are as follows: In the first place, you must have a STRONG WHY. Secondly, you must have a clear vision or goal. This means that you must know where you currently are, what your situation is, and where you plan to go. Thirdly, you must have different aspirations, a different mindset, and a different attitude than the rest of the crowd that you used to hang out with. You must be willing to differentiate yourself from others that do not share your dream, and above all, you must aim high, and must be laser focused. Moreover, you must be willing to study to show yourself approved, and you must be convinced in your mind that you deserve to be wealthy. Above all, you must believe in yourself and not give up. Let us consider all these qualities, one by one.

HAVE A CLEAR VISION

According to Webster's Dictionary, *vision* is the act or the power of anticipating that which may come to be. It is the ability to think about and plan for the future. You must know what it is that you want in life, and what you want to accomplish. The Bible emphatically says that without vision, the people perish. Why will the people perish? It is because some people don't know where they are, and they don't know where they are headed. If that is you, you must step back and look at your why. Is your why significant and robust enough? Is it compelling enough; is it convincing enough? Will you feel accomplished if you attain that goal? The importance of having a clear vision is because you want a clear-cut direction. So, if you're going to become a realtor, for example, then what you need to do is to know the steps involved to get there. Please take time now to develop a Vision Statement. After it is completed, make a conscious effort to move towards your vision.

ATTITUDE MATTERS

Besides having a clear vision, you must also change your perspective. Some people think that as soon as they jump into real estate, they will begin to make money immediately. Whereas that may be true in some rare instances, I will be the first to tell you that I have failed several times in real estate. However, I did not allow the failures to affect me negatively. I refused to let anything tie me down or mess with my mind or attitude towards my business.

In this line of work, attitude matters. You must have a healthy and positive attitude. You must change your way of thinking. You must change your way of walking. What do I mean by changing the way that you walk? Many people look down whenever they are walking, just because they have encountered some difficulties or failures. They feel ashamed of themselves. However, before you sink into the sea of despondency, I would admonish you to look at some of the great presidents who made it in life. Some of them failed several times before they became presidents. They refused to allow their past failures to determine their future successes.

Attitude matters because, whenever you fail, you must pick yourself up, learn from that experience, and strive hard to turn that failure into success. This is not the time to isolate yourself. This is not the time to ignore all your friends and business associates. You must have a healthy and positive attitude because, no matter what you go through or face in life, you must count it as a stepping-stone to achieve more successes. I don't know of any successful person that has not failed. If you are afraid of failure, you will never become wealthy.

AIM HIGH

With a positive outlook on life, you must *aim high* if you want to become successful. You cannot plan an average life and expect to achieve more significant goals. To become a successful real estate investor, you must be willing to do what ordinary people would not do. I used the word, *ordinary*, because ordinary people are satisfied with the status quo. For you to aim high and achieve greater things, you must be willing to break the rules of the average man. Sometimes you may have to get up very early, and go to bed very late. You may sometimes have to make that phone call that you would not ordinarily make. You must be willing to go beyond the call of duty. To aim high, you must be willing to take several risks. You must be willing to sacrifice. Do not settle for less, for the sky is the limit to what you can accomplish.

THE POWER OF FOCUS

Developing positive habits will help you to get far. Without the right practices, you will not get far, and will quit, and you will stop prematurely. It's just as simple as that. Determine the things that you love and are good at, and do ONLY those things. If you do not like filing, then don't do it. Do not waste your precious time on filing. Instead, look for someone who is best at filing, and have him or her do your filing for you. This would free up your time to do what is essential and most important in your business. You must look for things that steal away your time, and avoid doing those things. It doesn't matter how small that thing might be; it is a time waster.

Unless you want to appear busy, even though you are not creating value for the marketplace, then that is a different story. Many people think that they are making a difference by staying busy and doing mediocre jobs that pay about $5.00 per hour. That does not necessarily mean that you are working on your business. It says that you have a job, and you are very busy working in your business, rather than working on it. You don't want that. Your focus must be clearly identified, and it must be substantial. Once you have achieved that, you must take the necessary steps, each day, towards your goals.

One of the things that would help you to stay focused is *organization*. When you are organized, you take control of your time. By taking control of your time, you can manage your energy, thereby focusing on the things that matter and are necessary, and would pay you the most money. When you are laser focused, you work only on those activities that will bring success to your business.

You must be very careful about how you use your time. There are those that we call DREAM THIEVES. These are the people that are bent on stealing away your dream. They are bent on making sure that you stay in their inner circle, and that you do not grow or cut loose from them. They are determined and are sometimes very treacherous. They could be your peers, friends, family members, or even some self-proclaimed righteous mentors who are very poor and have achieved nothing in their own lives. These people will tell you that you will not make it, and that you will not amount to anything. They follow the average life and can see no way out of it. They probably have a little education, got married, had children, got a job, and live from paycheck to paycheck. Such people complain and find fault with anyone that tries to make it, and to make it big. STAY AWAY FROM SUCH PEOPLE. We call them THIEVES.

Contrary to the above, there are those who would support you through fires, floods, and tears. They are the *propellers*, or *the wind beneath your wings*. These are the people who will cheer you on and support you any way they can for you to succeed. I call them your CHEERLEADERS. You must be able to differentiate those who are eager to help you, from those who want to criticize you so that you do not succeed. I have been there and have done that. You need to surround yourself with like-minded people: those who understand your vision, and your why, and know that you want to accomplish something monumental. These people will support you and be there for you, even in times of difficulty. Spend your energy on such individuals, and do not waste your time on negative people. Always surround yourself with positive thinking people, who are going somewhere.

I said, earlier, to concentrate ON your business, not IN your business. By working in your business, you end up doing the mundane tasks that you are not good at and do not love, but waste time being busy. Do whatever it takes and is essential to grow your business. Believe it or not, you are not the best at everything that you do. I am sure there are myriads of things that you cannot do. By differentiating your weaknesses from your strengths, and by focusing on your strengths rather than on your weaknesses, you will save yourself a lot of time, stress, and worry, to spend on your business.

I watched the basketball championship game between San Antonio Spurs and Miami Heat (2013). It was this nail-biting championship game that brought the championship to Miami Heat. The most striking thing that is pertinent here is the fact that, of all the players that walked to the stadium to play, not

Why Real Estate

one of them carried the basketball hoop, the net, or even the basketballs from the locker room. I did not see any of the players placing a basketball pole in the ground and solidifying it before they played.

What I observed was shocking. By the time the team got to the stadium, the basket court was ready. It was clean. The basketball pole was already in the ground and very secured. The basketball hoop was already on the pole. All the benches for the spectators were lined up perfectly, and were ready and secured for the spectators. None of the players, not even those that sat on the bench throughout the game, did anything to the basketball court. Neither LeBron James or Duane Wade of Miami Heat, nor Tony Parker or Tim Duncan of San Antonio Spurs, assisted in digging holes to place the basketball pole in the ground. I did not see them getting on the ladder to set the net on the basketball hoop.

All they did was what they love to do. THEY PLAYED BASKETBALL. That is what gave them energy. I am sure that they spend a lot of time fine-tuning their game by practicing, lifting weights, and probably jogging. How about you? My question to you is this. As you embark on the game of real estate, are you going to be doing the things that sap all your energy: fixing toilets, mowing lawns, changing locks, painting, cleaning, or— like LeBron James—are you going to instead focus on your game and do what you love, so that you could be crowned with the title, MVP of Real Estate? I hope so. This is my prayer for you.

BE PREPARED: STUDY, STUDY, STUDY!

Over the years, I have realized that no matter how high I move on the entrepreneur ladder, it was my duty to keep studying and learning all the time. The reason is that the marketplace keeps evolving. The scriptures give a wonderful counsel in this aspect. *"Study to show yourself approved unto God, a workman that needs not to be ashamed, rightly dividing the word of truth."*

Attending seminars, reading books in your field, and familiarizing yourself with current events is key to your success. I have had mentors that guided me, and provided me with roadmaps, as I travel this road to success. Ask me again, and I will tell you that I still have mentors that I pay much money to, to guide me and share some of their wisdom with me. There is no one time that you should think that you have arrived and, therefore, do not need a coach or a mentor. I observe Tiger Woods exceedingly, and I admire his skills set, his mental toughness, and his focus on the golf field. Despite the number of times that he won the Masters, and despite all the skills that he possesses, he still has a coach that helps him to up his game.

I have a coach in every aspect of my life, because they support and guide me along the success paths that I travel. As you may be aware, the field of real estate keeps changing. Foreclosures, short sales, loan modifications, forbearances, credit score requirements, and a host of other unforeseen circumstances, play a vital role in real estate. Without studying, getting yourself updated, reading to familiarize yourself with what is going on in our world today, you may continue to implement old ideas, and you will be left behind. So, study, study, study; attend seminars, not to become a frequent seminar attendant but to learn the roadmap to success.

BELIEVE IN YOURSELF AND DON'T GIVE UP

Above all, you must believe in yourself. Without a firm belief in yourself, you are bound to fail. If you do not think that you will succeed, you are right. You will not succeed. It is just that simple. Have faith in God, and trust that He will guide you to become successful. Many people have limiting beliefs. They talk down to themselves and wonder why they cannot make it in life. If you tell yourself that you are stupid, then guess what? That is just how you will see yourself, and that is how you will operate. If you say to yourself that you cannot make it, guess what? You will not make it. However, if you believe that all things are possible, and that you deserve to be successful, your brain and your psyche will work towards success. People go through life in circles, without focusing on what it is that they want to accomplish in life. With that negative attitude, they live in despondency, and live a defeated life daily.

However, if you believe that you are a millionaire, you will strive to become a millionaire, and no amount of failures will bring you to a halt.

After I quit my job and decided to become a full-time real estate investor, the opposition that I faced was fierce: relatives, friends, colleagues, self-proclaimed and uninvited well-wishers, scolded me and laughed me to scorn. They said that I made a huge mistake. Not one of them offered to pay my mortgage, buy me food, or pay a portion of my utility bills for me. Not even once. My struggles were my own. My failures were my own. My deficiencies were my own. These individuals, however, had the nerve to give me their heartfelt and caring counsel to deter me from going after my dream and vision. If I didn't believe in God, and had doubted myself, I would be wallowing in my failures, and I would be stuck in the corporate world. Believe that you can make it, and you will make it.

So, my question to you is this: "What are you afraid of? What is it that keeps you awake at night? If you search within yourself, what are you worried about? What is it that is stopping you from moving forward? I started dreaming of becoming a real estate investor when I was in my teenage years. I completely lost track of myself, because I did not believe initially that I was capable of making it happen. I, therefore, decided to take detours on this journey. I went to college and secured an accounting degree, after which I clutched a job as an auditor. I lived from hotel to hotel because I was always on the road traveling. Although I was doing well, I thought that something was still lacking. I was unable to buy my own house, even though I wanted a home so badly. I was stuck. I was poor and did not realize it. What did I do? I started to justify, at the time, my state of poverty, by forcing myself to accept my situation just because I had my car.

However, guess what? Meanwhile, my parents were aging, and I was not able to help them financially, as I would have loved to at the time. This was a mind-blowing event for me. Despite all this, I did not realize that I had to rise above the frail to begin my own business. Even something on the side, fetching me some money consistently, would have been enough at the time. The mind-blowing thing, as I look back, is that I never bothered to read about entrepreneurs. I never bothered to learn about successful people. I never bothered to learn about those who had the financial capabilities and made things happen. Instead, I was satisfied with my average life and the status-quo. Moreover, then, the unthinkable thing happened to me. I was fired. I was not fired because I was not doing a good job; I was fired because my manager decided to hire a friend of his who had just lost his job. No matter how much money I made for the company, it did not matter. All the articles that I wrote for the company, on internal controls, did not matter. I then realized that I was just a number—an ordinary number—in the eyes of my boss. Also, I realized that my manager did not care about me like I thought he did. I thought I was his friend. I thought I was one of his top employees. I thought he was happy with my work, since he consistently gave me positive reviews of my performance.

Here I was, in the prime of my life, with an accounting degree and no job. I did not have any relative to call upon to help me financially. I did not have a wealthy father to send me money. I did not have a wealthy uncle to pay my mortgage. I was on my own—single, broke, and despondent. It was at this low point in my life that I decided to go back to school. As you can see, I did not learn my lesson to begin my own business. Instead, I enrolled to go back and pursue an MBA. Don't get me wrong. I am thrilled that I was able to go back to school to acquire my MBA. My only regret is that when I went back to school for my MBA, I did not have the guidance that I should have received from the experts. I did not have the opportunity to read the books on entrepreneurship either. If only I had read the books on entrepreneurship—if I had researched the life of successful people; if I had made up my mind to follow the footpaths of the real estate gurus—my focus at business school would have been different. I would have studied real estate or entrepreneurship. Then I would not have been so upset with my finance professor, who asked me to go into the corporate world, represent my business school very well, and make lots of money for my company.

I am sure that as you read this book, you may have a lot of fears and doubts as to whether you can make it. What I want to get across to you is for you to awaken that loud voice in you, that unstoppable voice within you that tells and convinces you that you are unique. That voice that keeps saying to you to come out of your shell and to stop hiding. The voice that continually nudges you and yells at you, and tells you that you can make it. That spirit that will not shut up, no matter how many times you tried, but keeps taunting you and keeps telling you that you are more significant than you think you are. That you are more powerful than you see yourself; that you are more capable than you see yourself, and that you are more authentic than you think you are. That spirit, that voice, that something that lies within you — I will urge you not to develop a deaf ear to whatever that thing may be.

You see, I do not know what your religious affiliation is, or even if you believe in God or a different higher power. One thing I know is that when you place your incapabilities, inadequacies, fears, and feebleness into the hands of God, when you put your dreams, your aspirations, and your goals in His hands, believing and trusting that He will lead, guide, and direct you, you will not go wrong. What is it that you have to do? Be diligent, be ready, and be prepared to do whatever it takes, and you will win.

CHAPTER 2

EFFECTIVE STRATEGIES FOR DEALING WITH CLIENTS

"Trust is the glue of life. It's the most essential ingredient in effective communication. It's the foundational principle that holds all relationships."
– Stephen Covey

THE CUSTOMER MATTERS

Whether you choose to go into residential or commercial real estate, please know that the customer is your number one priority. Your dealings with the customer can either make or break your business. You must treat them with respect. Treat them as kings and queens. I cannot emphasize this enough. Be fair in all your dealings with them. Some will drive you nuts. Some will tempt you to lose your patience, and you may feel like giving them a piece of your mind. Others will test you severely. No matter what the situation may be, you should develop the capability to treat them right. When you do this, you will win.

I am not advocating that you should become a doormat or a pushover, for your customers to walk all over you. That is not what I am trying to say. I want you to be firm and stable, and stand your ground, no matter what. However, in the midst of everything that you do, be conscious of the fact that the customer must be treated with the utmost respect. When you respect the customer, the customer will also respect you. They will realize that no one can push you around, and even if they don't like you, they will respect you and start referring others to you for business. They will see you as a person with integrity, and not a *pushover*.

Because of my tenacity and love for my clients, most of my deals come from referrals, especially from customers that know my track record. In this industry, a number of clients have tried my patience, in every sense of the word. But, whenever a client is trying to upset me to the nth degree, I will initially ask him or her to kindly calm down so we could intelligently discuss the issue at hand. If they choose to be rude, I do whatever I can to maintain my cool. I listen to what it is that they need, and then do whatever I can to give them a WOW experience. Do not take anything personally. Treat your discussions with your clients as business conversations rather than personal attacks. When you don't make anything personal, you are bound to do exceptionally well in any situation that you may find yourself in. Because I take nothing personally, and treat my discussions as business conversations, I can go beyond the call of duty. For example, if you get a call for a shower that needs repairing, make sure that you fix it within 24 hours. As a side note, it would be advisable to have a handyman on call to handle these unforeseen contingencies for you, if you decide to manage your properties.

LISTENING TO THE CUSTOMER

The word here, is *listening*. There is a huge difference between listening and hearing. Listening to your customer is critical. It can revolutionize your business. Sometimes it pays to visit your properties and have a chat with your customers or tenants. It will help you to find out what may be going on with your clients. By visiting them and talking to them one-on-one, it does several things to your business:

1. Your clients will know that you care enough about them to take some time out of your busy schedule to visit with them and see what is working for them and what is not working.

2. Your clients will be candid with you regarding issues that they may or may not be satisfied with. It will also create the atmosphere or forum for the client to be at ease with you, and talk to you from the bottom of their hearts.

3. Your visitation will help you to read the body language of your customer, and know what he or she may be thinking. If you are inclined to do something that is not being divulged, this will be the best time to ask them.

4. By visiting the client, you will create a bond. Hopefully, a positive one that will last for months and years to come.

5. Your customers will feel valued by you when you visit and listen to them, and will appreciate you as someone who genuinely cares about them.

A lot of people would *hear* what the customer has to say, but will not *listen* to them. This is a massive problem for some investors. You should try, at all costs, to avoid making such errors. If you don't listen to your customer so you can supply them with what they want or need, you will end up losing them. I look at the relationship between a landlord and a tenant as a parent-child relationship. Whenever a child comes to the parent, it is because that child trusts and believes that the parent would meet their needs at hand. If the requirement of the child is not satisfied, he or she will whine, cry, and express his or her disappointment and frustration, in varied shapes and forms. So it is with the customer that comes to you. You must do whatever it takes to satisfy that need. Once you fulfill that need, they will not look at your competition and have second thoughts about you. Instead, you will receive compliments that may win you other customers, just because you listened to them and took care of their needs.

Also, you must be willing to provide your customers with the service that your competition will not ordinarily give to their customers. A lot of landlords, for instance, believe in cutting corners. My best advice for you is to stay very far away from doing that. Instead, do whatever it takes to make the customer happy. Some landlords, without fail, will use inferior materials to replace damaged items that the tenant had complained about. It is not to say that you should use the most expensive things in the world to repair whatever is broken. Instead, give your customers WOW experiences every time. What I am proposing here is to *do unto others as you would have them do unto you.*

What you don't want is to wake up one day and face the real fact that your customer has decided not to do business with you any longer, because you did not rise to the occasion. As you may realize by now, clients like positive results. Your task at hand must be to focus on the customer and their satisfaction. The question that you need to ask yourself is: "Am I creating value for my customers, or am I just interested in collecting rent?" Are you different from other landlords, or are you just like them? Is there anything that differentiates you from others in the industry, or are you just like them? Remember, a happy customer or a satisfied client will always be motivated to treat your property with care. One thing that you must also realize is that your customers will stick with you if you treat them like they matter.

PROVIDE QUALITY WORK AND EXCEED EXPECTATIONS

Working in the corporate world has taught me some vital lessons. Every year, when I was with corporate, we had what was called *Annual Reviews*. This exercise was necessary for every employee to know where they stood with their manager or with the company: how the manager or supervisor perceived them, and whether the employee was still looked at favorably or unfavorably. I remember that the annual reviews were categorized as follows: Below Expectation, Meets Expectation, and Exceeds Expectation. Falling under any of these categories depended on my accomplishments for that year. If I did just okay, it was categorized as Meets Expectations. If, on the other hand, my accomplishments wowed my boss, I received an Exceeds Expectation grade. My promotion also depended on the quality of work that I provided. My presentations to senior management must be without flaws. I made it a point to review my submission to senior management, over and over again. I made sure that I knew my game very well, and knew what my argument was about. I anticipated the questions that would be asked by senior management, before they asked. I also made sure that I had answers to the problems before they asked the questions. Not being able to answer and defend my arguments, budgets, forecasts, or proposals was detrimental. Like the corporate world, our clients expect us to provide them with quality work.

So, if there are repairs that you need to undertake, be sure to WOW your client through the materials and the quality of work that you provide. Go to Home Depot, Lowes, or any other home repair store, and look for a quality showerhead that is neither cheap nor too expensive, and have that installed for your tenant. If you don't know what a quality showerhead is, then ask someone in the store, and they will help you to choose one. You must provide quality work that you will be proud of. Do not just fix broken items with cheap materials and then expect your tenant to give you an Exceed Expectations grade. You will end up receiving a Below Expectation or a Meets Expectation grade. If you want to receive an excellent grade all the time, then you need to be consistent by providing quality work. Strive to stay away from poor, inconsistent, cheap, or mediocre work. Always do your best so that you don't meet expectations but exceed expectations all the time. Do you want to know the gospel truth? Your clients are continually reviewing you. Let them talk about you. Let it be that among your competition, there is no one like you.

When you provide quality service to your clients, your business will excel. Do you know what happens when you do that? The word will spread about you. Other clients will hear about the kind of quality service that you provide for your tenants or clients, and your perfect name will spread like wildfire. It will generate more business for you, and your phone will start ringing off the hook. I have experienced this over and over. Currently, I have a waiting list of tenants that want to get into one of my properties. The reason is that they realize that I am not just like the others. Whenever a client needs something, we provide it with speed; that is as soon as possible. If it is not according to their satisfaction, then we do whatever we can to rectify the issue and make sure that we exceed the expectation of the customer.

It is sad to say that many businesses in this industry struggle to improve upon the kind of services that they provide for their clients. Rather than correcting their mistakes, they get angry or annoyed with the tenant, which sometimes results in the loss of the client. It has caused some businesses to take hits, whereby there's no growth but stagnation. They are not able to retain customers, tenants, or clients for a long duration of time. Providing lousy quality of service to your clients should be avoided at all costs. If not, you will drive several tenants or customers away from you. My advice to you is that if you provide service to a customer, which you are genuinely convinced that it is the best thing that you could have done for that customer, but the customer is not appreciative and complains, please do not take it personally. Find another way to rectify the issue, and give them what they asked for. When you give the customer what they need, your business will explode.

LANDLORDING

I remember when I acquired my first property. I was so excited that I didn't know what to do with myself at the time. I went to the extent of calling some of my friends to tell them that I had launched my first deal; especially all those who discouraged me from getting into this kind of business. Guess what? I bought my second property, then the third one, and a fourth one, and the rest is history.

As you embark on this journey of real estate, you too will be excited when you acquire your first property. The second one is

Effective Strategies for Dealing with Clients

as exciting as the third one, but as you purchase numerous properties, you will realize that you are not able to handle all of them by yourself. Acquiring properties is one thing, but the management of properties is a different animal altogether. Why do I say this? I have learned my lessons over the few years that I have been an investor. The University of Hard Knocks taught me valuable lessons, which I want to pass on to you. I do not want you to experience the same uphill battles that I had to struggle with. Management of your properties can be a very tasking and daunting ordeal.

Remember what I said earlier on: you must work *on* your business. Do not work *in* your business. If you decide to manage your properties, you will end up working *in* your business. The calls from tenants to fix broken items, locating tenants, cleaning up toilets, listing properties, marketing properties, the calls from you to remind tenants to pay their rent, the task of issuing eviction notices, etc.: all these can be classified as working *in* your business, as opposed to working *on* your business. When you spend your valuable time doing that which matters to your business—when you do the things that will propel your business—and restrain yourself from undertaking the $10.00 per hour jobs, then you are working *on* your business.

I can hear you loud and clear. Your question is how I go about these kinds of issues. I have an answer for you. Hire a property manager, or a property management company.

A property manager, or a property management company, is

one that is hired by the owner of the property to handle the day-to-day operations on his or her behalf. In return, the property manager is paid a fee, a salary, or a percentage of the rent that they collect. It doesn't matter the kind of property. It could be commercial or residential.

Some of the responsibilities of the property manager are as follows:

- Fill vacancies when a tenant moves out, or when you purchase a new property
- Set rent amount for the property
- Collect rent when it becomes due
- Issue eviction notices when a tenant defaults
- Deal with tenants' issues and complaints
- Screen tenants before they occupy the property
- Take care of the maintenance to ensure the safety and happiness of the tenants
- Take deposits on rent, in some instances
- Make the mortgage payment on a timely basis
- Keep accurate records of the property (know all income and expenses)
- Make sure that the taxes and insurance are paid on time (if not included in mortgage)

Payment of taxes on the property is severe and crucial. If you default, be sure to approach the county and make a payment arrangement to bring the balance current. If you choose to ignore it, and the taxes accumulate, your property may end up going to a tax lien sale, where you will lose the property. Please do whatever you can to avoid that from happening to you.

A couple of sources that I have researched for property management are www.irem.org, and www.npma.org. Either one of these websites can help you to locate outstanding property management companies that will take care of some of the daunting tasks, which you need not involve yourself with in the first place.

If you decide not to go with my advice on hiring a property manager, then my best opinion for you is to form a team of professionals who can support you. Following are some of the things that you must do if you decide to either rent or sell the properties yourself:

- Clean the property
- List the property
- Market the property
- Send out mailings about the property
- Answer calls from potentially interested parties
- Answer questions about the property
- Screen interested parties
- Show the property
- Collect deposits

HIRE YOUR OWN CLEANING CREW

After you have acquired the property, the chances are that the property may look filthy, and would require cleaning. Hire a professional cleaning crew. Not just anybody can go into a property and clean it up thoroughly and get it ready for renovation. It is, however, not your responsibility as a real estate investor to be cleaning your properties. One of the questions that you have to ask yourself is this: "What am I worth per hour?" If you answer that you are worth more than a hundred dollars an hour, then by all means, cleaning your properties is not your business. Have someone who will be satisfied with $15–$20 per hour to clean the properties for you. I can tell you that they would do a much better job than you. If you don't know where to get a cleaning crew to clean your properties, call the Chamber of Commerce in your city, or post the job on www.Craigslist.com.

HIRE A HAULING COMPANY

In specific instances, the city or the county where you live may have what is known as *bulk pick-up service*. It is where the city would dispatch a huge trash truck to pick up bulk items from your property or real estate. It is generally a free service that is offered by the city, to collect trash or unwanted bulk items that are left in the house by a previous tenant or a former owner of the house in consideration. When it comes to picking up things, for example, in Columbus, Ohio, the city is particular as to what they will pick up and what they will not pick up. If the items you have are remodeling items— for example, drywall or plywood (2 x 4s) that was used to renovate a house—the city will not pick up these items.

It is your responsibility to call the city to schedule the time to pick up the items. The kind of truck that the city will dispatch to pick up your items after you call them will depend on the number of things that must be collected from your property. Usually, they would like to know the descriptions and quantity of items that you are scheduling for pickup. Should the city or county not have bulk pick-up service, it behooves you to contact your current waste management company. They will sometimes schedule a bulk pick-up service for a fee. Before they show up, they would sometimes ask for specifics of the items they would be picking up. They may also ask you to set up all the trash by the curb on the morning of the pickup. They may require you to bag or box every piece of garbage.

If all of the above suggestions fail, then, by all means, hire a hauling crew or a hauling company. They may charge you a fee to pick up your items. Following are examples of what a hauling crew or company may pick up and dispose of: old mattresses, and all kinds of appliances, computers, and furniture. They may also take care of yard waste removal, trash removal, construction waste removal, foreclosure clean outs, and waste disposal. In every situation, maintain a professional relationship with all your clients, including the hauling company.

DEALING WITH THE SELLER

After the rehab is completed, you have a decision to make. Do you market and sell the property yourself, or do you hire someone else to market and sell it for you? My experience has been that whenever I bring someone on board to market and sell the property for me, it moves faster. You may be tempted at times to market and sell the property yourself. Whereas that is okay, you are limited as to how to market the property, and it may take a longer time for you to either find a tenant or a buyer.

My suggestion for you is to hire a real estate company. If you decide to go with a real estate company, the agent will have access to the MLS system and other websites that you may not have access to. It will allow the real estate agent to list your property on multiple websites. The benefits of having your property listed on numerous websites are that several interested parties could locate your property faster, once it meets the specifications that they are in search of. The real estate agent will also help you to come up with professional pictures, which could be posted on several websites, as well as the wordings and descriptions that are necessary to move your property as fast as possible.

HIRING A SALES PERSON

If you decide not to use a real estate agent, you must consider hiring a professional salesperson with experience in real estate. This individual should have the expertise needed in marketing.

They should have the experience in marketing properties to tenants as well. Before you conclude on hiring this individual, below are some questions that you must ask the potential client:

1. What experience do you have in real estate?
2. How many houses have you rented or sold in the past 60 to 90 days?
3. What references can you share with me?
4. What kind of advertising will you be using for my properties?
5. What websites do you envision using for my properties?
6. How many properties are you currently working on?
7. How often do you plan to show the property, and are you willing to hold open houses?

It is essential to agree on how he or she is going to get paid once you decide to bring the individual on board. If you choose to pay commission, be sure to have it in writing, and stay within the confines of the law. In some states, individuals that are not the real estate owners and do not have a real estate license, may not be allowed to sell your property. Do your due diligence so you can stay within the confines of the law.

DEALING WITH THE BUYER

Once a potential buyer has been identified, please be sure to treat him or her right. If there is a deal breaker before the final documents are signed, make sure you satisfy that need so that you do not lose that potential tenant or buyer. Once the papers are signed and the keys have been turned over to the buyer, it would be nice to send your new clients some flowers or a particular gift card, to say thank you for purchasing your property. It will go a long way because, if friends of theirs need a house in the future, guess who they would refer that friend, aunt, sister, or brother to? This kind of gesture may help propel your business ahead of your competition.

Remember, everyone likes gifts. There is nothing like giving a new buyer a present just to say welcome to the neighborhood. Spend no more than $50. So, I urge you to make sure that once you close the deal, send a present to show your appreciation.

EXCEED YOUR CLIENTS' EXPECTATIONS

As a real estate investor, exceeding your clients' or customers' expectations should be your number one priority. You have to and must go beyond the call of duty if you plan to succeed and stay alive in this industry. Unfortunately, many investors have their focus all mixed up. They are concerned about how much money they can squeeze from buyers or tenants, and as a result, they lose sight of the fact that the customer must be treated right. If this is an expertise that you lack as an investor, then, by all means, get someone who can oversee this part of your business, so you can thrive.

With that said, let's consider some things that you may incorporate into your business so you can quickly make your potential clients happy, and regard you as someone they would

Effective Strategies for Dealing with Clients

recommend people to go to.

1. Be Flexible

    In today's world, people are very busy, and time is an extremely essential commodity, as you can imagine. If you know that there are documents that must be signed or autographed, and the client cannot meet you in person, have the flexibility to enable them to use modern day technology to accomplish the same goal. I have several real estate agents that work for me, and on many occasions, I am unable to meet and sign documents that are urgently needed. As such, they would send those documents, and I could sign them electronically. It has saved me so much time, and I have been able to respond expeditiously to accomplish goals.

2. Better Business Bureau

    Aside from Twitter, Facebook, and other social media sites that your clients may use to grade you, the Better Business Bureau is another place where your clients can inquire about your performance. With that in mind, you may want to exceed expectations in whatever you do, because your clients, or your tribe, may be eager to give you excellent or negative feedback to potential clients. You need to realize that the client expectation of you is enormous, and when you blow that opportunity, your chances of gaining their trust back may become slim to none.

COMMUNICATION

Another area where you need to exceed expectation as a real estate investor is in the field of communication. This critical criterion that spells success is typically looked at as trivial, and as a result, ignored by investors. Miriam-Webster defines communication as *a process by which information is exchanged between individuals through a conventional system of symbols, signs, or behavior*. As an investor, you need to know your clients personally, if at all possible. These days, you can easily communicate with your clients through email, telephone, social media, etc.

Another reason why you need to communicate with clients is the importance of knowing where you stand with them. I ask my clients for feedback all the time. Guess what? They tell me like it is. They do not sugar coat or hide their feelings. Sometimes the feedback is what I would like to hear, and sometimes it isn't. But even in those instances, I am grateful, and I immediately rectify the situation that caused them to be unhappy. Once I right what was wrong, I don't leave it there. I ask if there is anything else that I could do to create a five-star treatment for them.

AVOID CREATING UNHAPPY CLIENTS

To make sure that you don't create unhappy clients or tenants, you need to have someone answer phone calls, emails, or even tweets, within 24 hours. Create an open-door policy, and let your customers know that you can easily be reached. Remember: do unto others as you would like them to do unto you.

Another way to avoid creating unhappy clients is to anticipate their needs before they occur. That is, you need to understand what they need and the best way to satisfy that need. It will go a long way, and your tenants or clients will love you for it. They will have nothing but good things to say about you.

As you anticipate the needs of your client, it would also be good to find opportunities where you can exceed their expectations, despite the situation. This is where you can create an unforgettable experience that could never be quickly forgotten. Once investors understand that real estate is a *customer oriented industry*, then strategically and intentionally do your best to apply the above recommendations to make your customers happy. Once you accomplish this goal, you will be beside yourself with joy, which will translate into growth in your business. You will not only grow your business and meet expectation, but you will exceed them.

Now that you know YOUR WHY to get into the real estate industry, and now that you have learned the practical strategies for dealing with clients, customers, and tenants, and now that you have learned how you can actually get referrals from your customers, because you have WOWED them and given them five-star treatments, I will teach you how you can actually find deals. Yes, race to Chapter 3, where I will show you how to find deals for your business. Indeed, we will be discussing this in Chapter 3, and we are going to talk about several vehicles that you can employ to find the hidden deals in the real estate world, which other investors can only dream about.

Go to Chapter 3, NOW!

CHAPTER 3

PROVEN WAYS TO FIND DEALS

"I have not failed.
I've just found 10,000 ways that won't work."
– Thomas A. Edison

One of the essential things to consider, when you get into the business of real estate, is the diverse WAYS TO FIND DEALS. Without good deals, there will be no business. Without good deals, you cannot make money. It is, therefore, essential to take this as a serious topic. The question is obvious. How do I find deals, or better yet, how do I find good deals that will profit me in this industry? Just before you get all hyped up and scared and negative, let me mitigate your fears. There are so many ways that you can find deals. Here are some suggestions and techniques that you can use to find good deals. If you don't do anything else but follow these directions, you would be on your way to creating wealth in the real estate business, in no time.

REAL ESTATE AGENT

One of the best sources for finding good deals is through the multiple listing systems (MLS). Unfortunately, the only ones that have access to this system are real estate agents. So, the question then is how do you get access to the system to find deals as an investor? This is where a realtor comes in. A real estate agent, or a realtor, is one that has attended a real estate school, and has acquired a state license to represent either a buyer or a seller in a real estate transaction. In return, the agent is paid commission for his or her efforts.

Working with real estate agents can sometimes prove very beneficial yet challenging for the real estate investor. It, therefore, behooves you as an investor to do your homework when it comes to finding a real estate agent that you can work with. It is not every real estate agent that understands what investors do. Real estate agents, as a whole, are concerned about the commission that they will receive after every transaction. The higher the sale amount, the better the commission they will receive. It is where I faced so many challenges in working with realtors. It was difficult for some of them to understand my formula for buying properties.

Some of the agents were extremely upset, just because I would not purchase what they thought was a good deal for me. If the deal did not make sense, I did not buy it. I did not care how beautiful the house looked. I did not care how great the location was. If it did not meet my buying criteria, I did not waste time going to look at the property. This initially got some of the real estate agents that I worked with very upset, and they stopped working with me. I am telling you this so that you don't lose hope once you begin to work with realtors.

My advice to you is that before you hire a real estate agent, you need to know what exactly it is that you are looking for. You need to know which area (location) you want to invest in. You need to know what your criteria for buying properties are. Sit yourself down and ask the obvious but fundamental questions: Are you interested in distressed (fixer-upper) homes, or are you just interested in properties that need only tender loving care (TLC)? What repairs can you tolerate, and what repairs are you not willing to handle? Can you afford to paint the whole house, should that be needed? How about flooring? Do you want to tear out the carpet and reinstall new carpet? Are you prepared to install new tiles or wooden flooring? How about plumbing? Are all the pipelines in excellent shape, or do they need work? Do you want to go through the expense when it comes to replacing new cabinets in the kitchen? These are a few questions that you have to ask yourself before you bring a real estate agent on board.

Once you are settled in your mind, and have answered these questions truthfully, pick up the phone and call a real estate office. You can call HER, or RE/MAX, or any real estate office of your choice, and ask to speak with a real estate agent that has experience in dealing with real estate investors. The reason this inquiry is necessary is that not all real estate agents know what investors want. Some agents cannot work with you if your offer is much lower than what they anticipated. To the agent who has no experience with investors, they would be insulted by offers that you make on deals that they bring to you. If your offer is much lower than what they expected, they will begin to question your seriousness. Your offer must come in a certain way to be acceptable. However, this is where you must stick to your guns as a real estate investor, and not allow yourself to be taken easily. You may ask why this is the case. The simple answer is that some realtors do not understand how investors work. All that they want is their commission. They are not interested in how much money you expect to make from a deal, but rather the commission they hope to make from a deal they bring to you.

So, be sure that there is a good understanding of what you need. Also, it would help if you give them your buying criteria, as well as your formula for buying. Once you find a real estate agent that has enormous experience with real estate investors, there are some critical questions that you must ask before you hire them.

1. Do you have experience working with real estate investors?
2. Do you invest in properties yourself?
3. How many investment properties do you currently own?
4. How long have you been investing?
5. What are some of the challenges that you face from your properties?
6. Are you willing to make multiple offers on my behalf?
7. Are you ready to bring me great deals, such as cash buyer deals?
8. Are you willing to accept a deferred commission or discounted commission until the deal is completed?

9. Can you submit comps and market analysis on each property that I am interested in?
10. Are you willing to give me a ballpark figure on repairs?

If the answers to these questions are affirmative and acceptable to you, then you can rest assured that you have found yourself an excellent real estate agent that will be willing to work with you. Such a realtor may bring you good deals, especially if you are committed to buying fast and closing quickly. The antidote is to do what you say you are going to do. Sometimes you may have to go through different or several real estate agents to find one that will work with you. Because of that, you may have a high turnover of realtors.

As I indicated above, the real estate agent is after his or her commission. That is how they get paid. So, be creative in your dealings with them. Be sure to honor your word and not deviate from what you promised to do. Offer them a commission when you buy from them, and then have them market and sell the property for you after you rehab it. In this way, they will be paid twice by you, because you offered them a double commission. At this point, they will not take you for granted any longer, and they will realize your seriousness in doing business with them. As soon as a deal hits their desk, guess who they will call first? It will be you. They will always look at you as that one investor that pays double commission, and they would be willing to continue to work with you.

MARKETING

Apart from a good real estate agent, there are various marketing techniques that you can use to find excellent deals, especially with motivated sellers. A motivated seller is one who owns the property but has become very tired of that property due to various reasons. A motivated seller could be a landlord who owns a single-family home, or an apartment building, but for one reason or another, doesn't want to manage or keep the property any longer. Another kind of motivated seller could be one who doesn't want to be in the real estate business any longer, and for that reason, would like to liquidate all the properties that he or she currently owns. It is not that hard to find motivated sellers, especially in this day and age, due to the influx of foreclosures all around us.

Let's look at a scenario. Let's say that John has a 30-year mortgage, from a reputable bank, on his gorgeous beachfront house in San Francisco. For the past five years, John has been very faithful in paying his mortgage on time, without being late, not even once. Then, one day, John got up and went to work as usual, only to find out that his job had been eliminated. At this point, John had no other source of income. Unfortunately, for John, he had no wealthy relatives that he could call upon to help him pay his mortgage. Let's say, although John had done whatever he could to secure another job, all his efforts had proved futile. Since John had not been able to pay his mortgage for the past three months, the bank—that John thought loved him so much—would, at this point, send him a *default letter*, reminding him of his obligation and his promise to pay his mortgage. If the fourth month comes, and John is still not in the position to pay his mortgage, the bank will, at this point, begin the foreclosure process to auction his gorgeous beachfront house, at a *sheriff sale*.

As you can see from the above scenario, John, the homeowner, is not only frustrated and stressed, but also very motivated to sell the property before the bank forecloses on it. In such a case, that becomes a deal for you, the real estate investor. We will be discussing short sales in another chapter. However, for now, let us stick to marketing.

Let us look at some of the various marketing techniques that you can use to generate leads:

DIRECT MAIL

This is when you send letters or postcards to homeowners, directly through the mail. I find *direct mailing* to be one of the most successful ways to get great deals. This type of marketing calls for creativity, and it is cost-effective. Let's look at some examples of direct mail:

Targeted Audience

One of the benefits to be derived from using direct mail is that you can choose a *target audience* that you want to send your mail to. For instance, you can choose to send your letter to a particular zip code, or to homeowners who are on the verge of facing foreclosure. What this means is that the homeowner is behind on the mortgage payment, but the bank has not yet foreclosed on the house. Another term for this type of lead is known as *pre-foreclosure*.

Absentee Owners

You can also target what we call *absentee owners*. An absentee owner is one who owns a property in a different city or state from where the owner currently resides. On many occasions, because the owners are absent from their properties, they would hire what is known as a property manager to take care of their home on their behalf. Such situations sometimes become very dicey, whereby the homeowner is not being treated right by the property manager that they have hired to take care of the property. This happens when the property manager collects the rent and then claims to use almost all of the rent money for what I will term as *fictitious repairs*. This, of course, creates distrust between the property manager and the absentee owner. When this continues, the house has become a liability to the owner, and as a result, he or she becomes motivated to sell or get rid of the property.

A direct mail from you at this point would go a long way because you have just become one who could rescue them from their misery. They'll be so inclined to respond to you immediately. They will also see you as the one wh0 has been able to identify their problem and provide a solution. They would be so inclined to deal with you, and turn over their property to you without any hesitation.

It may interest you to know that my third deal was from an absentee owner. This couple lived about seven hours away from their property. Then they received a letter from me, letting them know that I was interested in purchasing their house. As soon as they received my letter, the couple called me immediately, and offered to meet with me the following day. To be honest with you, I was amazed that I received that phone call from them. I was not expecting them to meet with me at the designated time, because they told me that they lived about seven hours away. I began to question how this couple would travel to Columbus, Ohio to meet with me on the following day. This is a prime example of motivated sellers. Guess what? They drove all night to hand over the house, the deed to the house, and the keys, to me on the following day. I closed on the home, 30 days after the house was deeded to me. To date, I still own the house. This is what direct mailing to an absentee owner can do for you.

PROBATE/INHERITED PROPERTIES

Probate is a process where a court decides on whom to assign the responsibility for assets of an estate. It is a legal process that is supervised by a court, in administering the estate of someone who has died. This could be a parent or a grandparent, or another relative. The reason or the purpose of this kind of process is to be sure that the obligations or debts, including taxes owed by the deceased before his or her demise, are taken care of or paid by the beneficiary. This means that all unpaid debts are transferred to individuals who are entitled to inherit the estate in question.

So, the question is, how do you, the investor, get access to these kinds of deals? My answer is that you have to use a direct mailing campaign, by sending direct mail or a postcard to the one that has been assigned as an executor handling the probate for the deceased family member, or to the probate attorneys. As you can see by now, there is quite a lot of money to be made from these kinds of deals. One of the reasons is that you can purchase these properties below market value, since the sellers are very motivated to get rid of the inherited property to avoid family feuds that could later on emerge.

It may interest you to know that people who inherit probate properties are generally not expecting that kind of inheritance. The responsibility can sometimes create a burden for the relatives of the deceased, due to all the legal ramifications. As a result, many of the children of the deceased end up being motivated and, therefore, would quickly sell the property rather than hold it and incur a lot of expense trying to fix it so they could sell it at a later time.

DIVORCE ATTORNEYS

Another source of direct mail that I have used, which I find very beneficial, is to couples who are facing divorce. You may be surprised that many couples on the verge of divorce are very angry at each other and, therefore, do not want anything to do with the spouse any longer. Because of that, they become so motivated that they want to get rid of the property that they currently own together. It is an excellent source of leads from motivated sellers. How do you find these kinds of deals? Send letters to divorce attorneys, letting them know who you are, what you do, and how you can help in resolving real estate issues very quickly for their clients. I will advise that you also let the attorney know that you would reward them nicely, as soon as you close on a deal that they bring to you. Please be true to your word, and send the attorney a referral fee. This would let the attorney know that you are someone that he or she can depend on, and would, therefore, start to send you several referrals as soon as they become available.

YELLOW LETTER

Whereas I cannot claim to be the one who created the *yellow letter*, I can tell you that I know the one who invented this brilliant idea. It happened that I was at a real estate function in Florida, and was getting some ideas about marketing for deals, when this guy (I will not mention his name) and his wife told me what they did the previous week, which resulted in an insane response, and continued to generate leads for them. They then gave me a sample of that yellow letter, for free, to try when I returned home.

So, what in the world is a *yellow letter*? A yellow letter is a handwritten letter, on a yellow sheet of paper, asking someone to sell their house to you. You can get a printer to have a bunch printed for you so that you do not waste too much time writing individual letters. I can tell you that it is not easy trying to write so many handwritten letters in a sitting. If you, however, decide to have the letters printed, be sure to ask the printer to use yellow or white, 8 x 12, lined paper, with an imitation of a handwritten letter, using red ink.

As soon as the letter is ready, have it neatly folded and placed in a non-legal sized envelope. The envelope has to be hand addressed as well, to give it a personal touch. Anyone who receives this kind of mail will automatically think that the letter is from a friend or a relative, and will immediately open it. The only ink that I have used is red, although others who have used black or blue ink testified positively to the number of leads that this letter brought them.

I must tell you that I have personally benefited tremendously from this type of direct mail campaign. If you take it seriously, the sky is the limit as to the number of responses that you will receive from the use of yellow letters as a direct mail campaign. Following is an example of the words that I place on the yellow letters that I send out:

Dear {insert the name of the house owner}

Hi,
My name is {insert your name}. My wife {insert your wife's name}

and I would like to
Buy
your house at:
 {insert property's address}

Please call me at {insert your telephone number}

Thank you,
{insert your name}

EXPIRED LISTINGS

Another good source of generating leads is sending direct mail to *expired listings*. This happens when a contract between a seller and a realtor no longer exists, because the contract for the listing of the home has expired, and the house did not sell. It gives you, the investor, an urge to locate homeowners who are desperate to sell their homes.

One thing that you must understand is that there are so many varied reasons why a house does not sell during the contracted period. It could be that the location is not attractive, or that the price of the house is too high, or that there may be repairs that the seller is not willing to undertake, etc. When the house does not sell within the contracted period, the seller becomes very stressed, anxious, and very motivated.

With this knowledge, it is essential for you to have access to the multiple listing (MLS) database, to find the listings that have expired. As I explained above, the ones with access to the MLS system are realtors. Therefore, be sure to contact a realtor with whom you have established a substantial relationship, to send you the expired listings.

Once you receive the listings, send a direct mail to the homeowners, explaining how you plan to buy their house and close on it quickly. Remember, some of these expired listings could be as a result of foreclosures, or due to relocation, divorce, probate, etc. Make sure you can close on it as promised, once the seller is willing to have you purchase their property.

FEDERAL EXPRESS ENVELOPE

When I receive a Federal Express envelope, I open it immediately to see the contents, who sent it, and the urgency for posting such mail to me. While opening it, I am always thinking about what may have inspired someone to send me that kind of mail. Since you are not Federal Express, or UPS, and do not have access to the Federal Express envelopes, what you can do is to purchase what is known as Federal Express envelope imitations.

You then send your direct mail in a mini Federal Express envelope, or a mini UPS envelope. It will get immediate attention. I can promise you that the receiver would not treat such envelopes as junk mail, but would be forced to open it out of curiosity to see what is in that package. Again, the idea here is to have your potential client open the mail.

Be mindful of the fact that some of these homeowners that you are targeting are being bombarded by other real estate agents and investors, who do not know what they are doing. You must, therefore, set yourself apart, to be different and creative, so that whenever a potential client receives your mail, they would be convinced about your qualifications and experience.

LUMPY MAIL

Lumpy mail is a letter that has a lump inserted in it, and is sent directly to a potential client. Lumpy mail is a direct marketing strategy that can improve your mailing campaign rates, and help you get deals above your competition, thereby realizing a considerable return on your investment. The reason why it's called *lumpy mail* is that it is indeed *lumpy*, in comparison with traditional *flat* mail. Unlike flat mail, lumpy mail is dimensional, and it is actually lumpy. This strategy works because it stands out from every other mail. Some of the items that you may consider inserting in the envelope could be a pen, a pin, a piece of nicely decorated two by four wood, or a small key holder, just to give you some ideas. It definitely serves as a unique way to grab a potential seller's attention to open the mail and respond back to you.

POSTCARD

Another form of direct mail that you may want to consider is the postcard. Although there are different sizes, a lot of people gravitate towards the 4 x 6 card, since it is believed to be roomy, and you can easily manipulate the words that go on the card. Others argue that the 4 x 6 is the best card to send because pictures look nice and professional on them. Other schools of thought think that it is better to use the regular postcard. It is your choice as to which one to use. Whatever your choice is, postcards are very inexpensive and can be an excellent marketing tool to generate leads for your business.

INVITATION ENVELOPE

This is another form of direct mail that causes people to open the letter. It is one of those marketing creativities that compels your potential client to open your mail very fast. The envelope looks like a party invitation, wedding invitation, graduation invitation, or a retirement invitation, that someone has extended to you for a special occasion. It creates excitement and anticipation by the recipient, which drives him or her to open the envelope to see what the invitation is all about. Again, the idea behind this is to have your letter opened.

INTERNET

There are several websites that you can go to get leads. Some of the sites that I will recommend are www.Craigslist.org, Realtor.com, Biggerpockets.com, and a host of other websites. Whenever you are on any of these sites, make sure you search for some keywords, such as *motivated sellers, must sell, foreclosures, pre-foreclosures, need to sell,* etc.

You may also want to look for categories such as *real estate for sale, real estate wanted, real estate by broker,* or *real estate by owner.* You can use any of these categories to generate leads for yourself. Once there, send an email to the seller or, if possible, pick up the phone and call the number that is listed with the posting. Let the seller know that you are interested in buying their property—for cash. Through your email or conversation over the phone, the seller needs to know that you are a serious buyer who can afford the property and can close as soon as possible.

SOCIAL MEDIA

The use of Social Media is enormous these days. In this fast-paced, technological world, it is crucial to use these social sites to generate leads. Following are typical sites that could bring you huge leads:

- Facebook Marketing
- Pinterest Marketing
- LinkedIn Marketing
- Twitter Marketing
- Snapchat Marketing
- Craigslist Marketing

BIRD DOGS

For real estate investors, one of the more traditional ways to look for leads is by using *bird dogs.* Bird dogs are human beings—not dogs—that you send out to search for or pursue properties for you. You, the investor, must spell out to your bird dog what your requirements are. For example, your requirement could be for the bird dog to look for vacant homes, distressed properties, abandoned homes, homes that have been destroyed by fire, or For Sale by Owner homes (FSBO). The property does not always have to be in bad shape.

Once a property is located, and meets your buying criteria, have the bird dog take a picture of the front and the side of the house, as well as the back and the roof, and have the pictures brought to you. In return, pay the bird dog for the picture(s) that he/she brings to you. Make sure that you negotiate before sending him/her out, so that there is no confusion as to the compensation once the pictures are delivered to you. I pay no more than $10.00 per picture that is brought to me. Before you say that the pay is too low, remember that you are not sure at this point if you're going to buy the property. Secondly, the bird dog saw the house and thought it might be empty, but it may not be a vacant house after all.

BANDIT SIGNS

Another tool that generates good leads, which you could implement, is *bandit signs*. It is old fashioned, but it works. One sign could bring you three to five houses. I am sure that as you drive around town, you have seen this kind of sign. It reads as follows: *We buy houses fast and can close quickly*. Alternatively: *Cash for your house in 9 days*. You can spot them on major roads, street corners, or at stoplights.

The signs are typically placed on poles, or sometimes on wires, or hammered to the ground. You can see them on the ground with telephone numbers. You cannot miss them. The word, *bandit*, refers to placing an ad on a plot of land that is not owned by the owner of the sign. These kinds of signs come in different sizes and colors. Let your printer know the exact size that you want and the colors that you are interested in.

The goal of the bandit signs is to have someone call you. My disclaimer is that in some areas, placing signs by the roadside could be illegal, even though it works very well. Whenever you put a bandit sign in the ground, chances are that it may remain there for a while. On other occasions, you will be asked to remove the sign. If an officer asks you to take it down, please do so. I have been asked before by an officer to show him the license that authorized me to place a bandit sign by the roadside. I respectfully told him that I did not have one. He then asked me to remove it. All this time, he parked his car behind me, waiting to see what I was going to do. I thanked him and immediately took it down. I made sure that I got back in my car after removing the sign, and drove off, leaving him sitting in his car. The last thing that you want to do is to get in trouble with the law. It is also advisable that you consult your attorney or call your city to find out if bandit signs for lead generation are allowed. If it is legal, please go ahead and use them; but if not, resort to one of the strategies that I have chronicled above.

I have been blessed over and over again by using bandit signs. If you are fortunate enough, the bandit sign that you leave on a pole will stay there for quite a long time before it is removed. Such was my case when I received a call from a lady asking me to meet her at her house so I could walk through the house, and purchase it if it fit my buying criteria. I asked how she had heard about me. She answered that about a month ago, she saw a sign that I had placed on a pole. She said that she took the number and had been wanting to call me every single day, but did not dare to call me since she believed it was a scam. I told her that it was real and not a scam. We set up an appointment immediately. Two hours later, I was at the house. Ten minutes later, I presented her with an offer, and because I was prepared with all my forms in my bag, she signed every single document that I carried with me, and she deeded the house to me on the spot.

Bandit signs are cheap, and can bring you many leads—today, tomorrow, and several months from now. Your focus is to be sure that many people see your sign. The more people that look at your sign, the more likely you will get a call from someone who is either facing foreclosure, divorce, or is just desperate to sell their home. If that happens, you have achieved your goal. If you are too busy or too shy to place the bandit sign yourself, I would advise you to outsource it. Find someone, perhaps a college student, to put up the signs for you. You can pay them the minimum hourly wage. You may want to do stop checks on them to be sure the signs are placed according to your instructions.

CLASSIFIED ADS

There is this floating myth going around that because the Internet has overtaken the world, not many people read the newspapers anymore. I'll be the first person to tell you that it is not true. Despite popular belief, there are a whole lot of people who continue to place ads in the newspapers today. With that said, you may want to look at classified ads in the newspapers. Whenever I buy the paper, I immediately look at the For Sale by Owner (FSBO) section, or Properties for Sale section. I go through them and call the individuals that have posted ads of their houses in the newspapers.

Common places to find good deals are in your community newspapers, the local newspapers for your city, or the newspapers that you see at the 7-Eleven shops. Some of the publications don't cost you any money. Pick up those newspapers and go through them. Go to the sections to see who may be motivated to sell you their home. I can tell you that I have gotten some good deals just from classified ads. One that I remember vividly well is a family that was going through some severe financial crises and could not afford to keep their house any longer. All they needed was a couple of thousand dollars to move out of the property. Because I was the first person to call them, I set up an appointment with them, and then followed up to go and look at the house on the same day. I offered them what they needed, and the house was immediately deeded to me. Within a couple of weeks, they moved out of the house. I was able to cure the debt, did the minor repairs, and rented it out during the same month. To date, I still own the house. This was just because of a classified advertisement that was placed in the papers, of which I had immediately taken action.

AUCTIONS

Going to auctions can sometimes prove profitable. There are so many types of auctions that are available. One of the auctions that most people are familiar with is the *sheriff's sale*. This is where the sale takes place on a particular day of the week, on the steps of the courthouse. In some areas, this is held on either Thursday or Friday. If you have the money and can pay cash, this could end up bringing you some great deals. To find out when an auction is taking place in your county, pick up the phone and call the courthouse, and ask for the sheriff's office. Ask them about the list of auctions that would be held during that week. Once you get the list and find a property that you may be interested in, go to the auction and bid on it.

Let me caution you, however, that before you go to the auction, make sure that you go through the list of all the properties that may be auctioned on that day. Again, do your due diligence. Find out about the after-repair value (ARV), by using comps. Know the location of the property, and be sure that you are comfortable with that. Find out about the current value of the property to see if there is enough room to make some good profit based on your buying criteria.

If possible, drive by the property, or have somebody else do that for you. This is good since it would give you an idea, at least from the outside, as to the structure, the roof, the gutters, if there are any trees, and whether the house is actually in overall good shape. If the house is vacant, you may want to look inside through the windows to get a general idea as to what you are up against. If it is not empty, do not go anywhere near the property, because you do not want to get in trouble by offending the people living in it. Remember, they are already angry that the bank or lender is foreclosing on them. Do not be a victim of someone's frustration.

Additionally, you may want to consider other Internet sites, such as eBay.com, or Auction.com, to bid on properties.

Other sources for leads are:

- Radio Advertisements
- Television Advertisements
- Vacant properties
- Title companies
- Realty Trac.com
- Eviction filings
- Tax Liens
- Miniature transfers

Now that we have discussed the various ways that you can locate great deals at length, race to the next chapter, where we will discuss in detail the VARIED WAYS TO ANALYZE DEALS ONCE YOU LOCATE THEM. See you in Chapter 4.

CHAPTER 4

PROVEN WAYS TO ANALYZE DEALS

"If the only tool we use to analyze what's valuable is a price tag, then those things that don't have price tags begin to look like they have no value."
– Al Gore

Making offers on any property can be very scary, yet exciting. It can be the most frightening thing on earth because, when evaluating deals, you have to know and understand your numbers. If you do not know what you are doing, it may end up costing you a lot of money, and may also cause you to leave quite a bit of money on the table—a very costly experience that you may not want.

One of the most important things that I want you to factor into your analysis is *due diligence*. What is due diligence, and why is it necessary? It is the steps required, or the process that you, as the buyer, must take to thoroughly investigate the property you are interested in acquiring, before you purchase it. I cannot express how crucial due diligence is; it will help you to remove or reduce the risk that may be associated with the property before you own it. If you forgo this critical process, you may be disappointed. The seller, on the other hand, may end up getting everything that he or she wants out of the property, and you will not have any recourse after you close on it.

Some of the items that you may want to consider during the performance of your due diligence are as follows: Have a professional do a video inspection of the sewer lines for any potential leaks or wear and tear. Check all the plumbing, the septic system, and the electricals. Also, be sure to check the statistics of crime in the area, the school district, and the quality of schools in the area. Besides, be sure that the location of the property is what you want. These are just a few examples of what you want to factor into your due diligence process.

If you miss out on this, it could cost you a serious amount of time and money. You need to know what essential items you want to include in your analysis. Be very strategic and intentional about this; or else you may end up leaving out some crucial elements that need to be factored into your analysis. Evaluating your deals based on factual numbers can help you tremendously to determine the real value of the property.

Conversely, analyzing a deal on a property can be exciting, because if you do your *due diligence* correctly, without leaving anything out, nothing can stop you from moving forward to acquire the property. You may uncover some things that could force the seller to reduce the price of the house. Unfortunately, there are a lot of new and some self-proclaimed professional investors that will not do due diligence when acquiring properties. It is very risky.

When it comes to analysis, be sure to include all the expenses that you incurred in acquiring the property, and the acquisition cost, as well as the amount of profit that you desire to make on a deal before jumping into it with both feet. For these, and many other reasons, I decided to write this chapter. It is just that crucial and beneficial. I know that if you follow my guidelines very carefully, you will save yourself a lot of headaches and worries, and will be able to determine the actual value of the property from different angles.

When analyzing a deal, you need to know the current value (CV) of the property. Also, you need to know the after-repair value (ARV). The after-repair value is simply the amount that the property will sell for after you have rehabbed or fixed it.

Once you have obtained the CV, as mentioned above, and the ARV of the property, it behooves you to know the *comps*. Comps are also known as *comparables*, or *comparative market analysis* (CMA). It is a tool or a system that is used mainly by real estate professionals—appraisers, title companies, real estate agents—to evaluate homes that have sold, or properties that are currently listed on the market, within a specific time frame, and within a certain mile radius. During the evaluation process, comps are used to evaluate the subject property by comparing similar size, condition, age, and style of recently sold or listed homes, in a targeted neighborhood or community. The primary purpose of using comps is to help you determine the fair market value for your subject property.

If you don't know how to get comps, ask your real estate agent. When using comps, you have to compare apples with apples, and not apples with oranges. In other words, are all the houses that are selling in the area, three-bedroom or four-bedroom dwellings? Do they have basements, fireplaces, one bath or two bathrooms? If your property is lacking in some respects, then adjustments would have to be made. Again, your real estate agent can help you with accurate comps. You may also want to consider doing an appraisal, or what is known as *brokers price opinion* (BPO), especially if the property that you are considering making an offer on is old.

REPAIRS

If you choose to work with a real estate agent, make sure the real estate agent gives you a high level of the competitive repair estimate. One of the touchiest parts of real estate evaluation involves the difficulty in estimating repairs. Your real estate agent will be able to identify problems that you may not see. He or she can also recommend a good home inspector that will provide a detailed report on the issues with the house.

If you are not using a real estate agent, then have your contractor give you an estimate on the repairs. This is very important because you want to include the cost of repairs in your numbers before making an offer on the property in question. Sometimes it is very good to factor in an extra 10% contingency, which would serve as a cushion just in case you miss some things that you have not factored into your estimated repairs.

OTHER COSTS

Other factors to include in your evaluation process are:

- Holding costs
- Inspections
- Taxes
- Insurance
- Utilities
- Real estate agent's commission

One of the ways of performing due diligence is by knowing the real estate formulas. If you walk in blindly, the chances are that you may come out okay, or you may end up losing a lot of money, and based on how you raise funds to buy the property, your investors, or even the bank, may not be too happy with you.

At this point in the evaluation process, let us consider some of the formulas that you may want to consider when buying your real estate.

FORMULAS TO CONSIDER WHEN EVALUATING DEALS

1. Maximum Allowable Offer (MAO) =

(ARV * 70%) - (Finance Costs + Repairs)

Let us take a house with an after-repair value of $200,000, finance cost of $5,000 and repairs of $15,000. Our goal is to calculate the *maximum allowable offer*. This formula will quantify the maximum offer that we want to make to the seller or owner of the house that we want to purchase.

Based on the above formula, an example of MAO is as follows:
MAO = $200,000*.70) - ($5,000 + $15,000)
MAO = $140,000 - $20,000
MAO = $120,000

More Explanation:

ARV: The *after-repair value* is the amount that you are willing to sell your house for, once the rehab is completed and is ready to hit the market.

MAO: This is the *maximum amount* that you are willing to purchase the property for. Not one penny more. If you deviate from this offer, you may end up losing money. (70% indicates that you are willing to offer 70 cents on the dollar for the property.)

2. Maximum Purchase Price (MPP) = (Sales Price - Fixed Costs - Expected Profit - Repairs)

Let us take a house with an after-repair value of $300,000, fixed costs of $20,000, repairs of $18,000 and expected profit of $25,000. Your goal is to calculate the maximum purchase price that you are willing to buy the property for.

Based on the above formula, the MPP is as follows:

MPP = $300,000 - $20,000 - $25,000 - $18,000

MPP = $237,000

3. 65% Rule

This is where you make an offer of 65% of the after-repair value to your seller. As you may have already observed, this formula is mostly used by investors who want to wholesale the property to another investor. This investor, or the buyer, may be interested in rehabbing the property to keep it as a rental. The secret behind this formula is for you, the wholesaler, to make a quick profit on the property. The strategy then is for you leave a lot of money on the table for the rehabber—in this case, your buyer. If you become too greedy and do not leave enough money or profit in the deal for the investor, you may be stuck with the property, and not be able to sell it for a while. You will be shooting yourself in the foot and will not be able to make that quick cash.

The 65% Rule factors in the profit that the wholesaler wants to make. So, if the after-repair value of the house that you want to buy is $100,000, then per the 65% Rule, the calculation of your offer will be as follows:

$100,000 x .65% = $65,000

Then $65,000 - $25,000 (Estimated Repairs) = $40,000

Then $40,000 - $5,000 (Assignment Fee) = $35,000

With this example, the offer that you will then make to the seller will be $35,000.

4. Net Operating Income (NOI)

This is the gross operating income less operating expenses in a given month.

Gross operating income includes:

The annual rent income plus any other income from other sources, such as coin-operated laundry facilities, vending machines on site, etc.

Operating expenses include:

- Maintenance
- Insurance

- Utilities
- Property taxes
- Repairs

(Do not add principal and interest, income taxes, insurance, capital expenses, and/or depreciation to expenses.)

5. Debt Service Coverage Ratio (DSCR)

This is a ratio that is used mainly in commercial real estate deals. It is principally used by commercial lenders to analyze how much a commercial loan can be supported by the cash flow that would be realized from a particular property (apartment complex); or to determine how much income coverage there is at a particular loan amount.

This ratio establishes the relationship of a property's annual net operating income (NOI) to its annual mortgage debt service (principal and interest payments).

So, let's look at a simple example of DSCR: If the subject property has $125,000 in net operating income, and $100,000 in an annual mortgage debt service, then the DSCR will be 1.25. 125000/100000 = 1.25

This formula tells me that you have a positive cash flow. At 1.00 you are at a break-even point. If, on the other hand, your calculation comes in less than a 1.00, then you had better seriously reconsider that property. That will be a negative cash flow, or a *net operating loss,* based on the proposed debt structure that you want to stay away from.

Expense Ratio or Operating Expense Ratio (OER)

This is the operating expenses divided by its revenues. I use this calculation in my analysis quite a bit, because it measures the costs associated with operating property, in comparison to the income that it generates.

The calculation is as follows: Operating Expenses / Revenues

For this formula, let us say that the property you are considering purchasing has a monthly operating expense of $5,000, and a monthly revenue of $25,000.

Based on the above formula, the calculation will be as follows:

Operating Expense Ratio = $5,000
$25,000 = 20%/month

Since operating expenses represent costs incurred while running the business, the more you can cut down on your expenses, the better you will be; therefore, the less your expenses, the more profit you will make on your property. You can use the above ratio, as a real estate investor, to compare properties that you may be interested in acquiring. So, stay away from properties that have a high operating expense ratio.

6. Cap Rate

Capitalization rate, or *cap rate*, as it is commonly called, is mainly used by commercial real estate investors. It measures the ratio of the net operating income (NOI) to the value of the property under consideration to purchase. In other words, it is a rate of return on an investment property, based on the projected income that the property will generate in a situation where cash is used.

As an example, if the property has a value of $750,000, with a net operating income of $49,872:

The cap rate would be $49,872/$750,000 = 6.6%

Capitalization Rate = Net Operating Income Purchase Price

Looking at another example, assuming you find a retail building with a cash flow of $500,000 (NOI), and a purchase price of $5,000,000, then the Cap Rate will be 10%.

Cap Rate– $500,000/$5,000,000 = 10%

So, what exactly does this mean? The cap rate gives us the returns that an investor would realize on a cash purchase price of a property.

Thus, an acquisition capitalization rate of 6%, versus a 12% capitalization rate for a similar property, will tell you that one property is riskier than the other.

The good thing about the above formula is that you can quickly solve for the value of a property. You can easily find the *value* of a property when you know the *net operating income* and the *cap rate*.

With that said, how will you quantify the value of a property when you have the cap rate and also the income? It will be as follows:

Value = Net Operating Income/Cap Rate

So, a net income of $1,000,000, with a cap rate of 10%, will give us the following value of the property you are considering purchasing:

Value = $1,000,000/.10

The *value of the property* will be $10,000,000.

Whereas cap rate gives us useful information about a property very quickly, we also need to consider all the factors involved, especially where cash flow tends to fluctuate quite a bit. In such a situation, you need not leave out the necessary *cap rate modifiers*.

7. Cash on Cash Returns (CoCR)

This is the ratio that measures the anticipated cash flow to the amount of initial cash investment you made to purchase that particular property. So, your initial cash investment could be: down payment, points that you paid for, title fees that you paid for, inspection fees, and/or appraisal amounts that you paid for.

CoCR= Cash Flow Before Taxes/Initial Investment

For instance, let us assume that you found a property with a purchase price of $200,000, with a 20% down payment, and a net income of $15,000.

Based on the above formula, your *cash on cash return* will be as follows:

CCR = $15,000/$40,000 = 38%

8. Loan to Value (LTV)

Loan to value is that percentage of the property's value that is mortgaged.

LTV = Mortgage/Appraised Value

An example is as follows: A loan of $800,000, with a property value of $1,000,000, will give a *loan to value* as follows:

LTV = $800,000/$1,000,000 = 80%

Before you buy, make sure that you understand your *exit strategy*. Some of the strategies are as follows:

a. Hold and Rent
b. Retail (sell to end user)
c. Option

OTHER CONSIDERATIONS BEFORE YOU BUY

- *Exit strategy* is how you plan to get rid of the property once you buy it. You must decide what strategy you want to employ prior to making an offer. The question to ask yourself is, "What will I do with this property once I purchase it? Am I buying this property to hold, or am I buying it to immediately sell it to other investors?" This is just to give you some ideas as to the kind of strategy that you may want to think about before making an offer.

- Once you decide on your exit strategy, proceed to make your offer, and buy the property. I see a lot of real estate investors who don't think about their exit strategy. They proceed to make the offer and then think about what to do next. Do not fall into this category. A lot of real estate investors end up getting burned because they did not take the time to determine their exit strategy. If you do your homework well, chances are, you will come out just like you planned. If your exit strategy is to buy and hold, you will know exactly how to make the offer. But on the other hand, if you decide to rehab and sell, then your proposal to the owner of the property or the seller may be different.

- It is crucial for you to know your exit strategy before stepping into the deal. Knowing your exit strategy will dictate what funds to raise. You will also have an idea of the kind of properties to look for, areas to target, what offers to make, and how to make those offers. You will not waste time chasing dead-end leads. Let's look at some examples of exit strategies:

WHOLESALING

Wholesaling is when you purchase a property but decide to sell it to someone else without repairing or fixing the property yourself.

You can do this in three different ways:

1. You place a property under contract, and then sell it to a potential rehabber or investor before you close on it. When this happens, you will engage in what is known as *double closing*. This means that although you placed the property in a contract, you will not use your own money for the deal. You will sell the property to someone else, who will then bring the amount of money that you are requesting for the property, to closing. In this scenario, you are the seller of the property. Your buyer will need to bring the money to the

title office or to the attorney's office, where the closing is to take place. The money that he uses to purchase the property from you is what you will end up applying to close on the deal. Your profit is the difference between the amount that you are selling the property for, and the purchase price that you negotiated the property for, from your seller.

Following is an example:

- Seller A sells his house to you, the investor, for $100,000.
- You (the investor) then sell the same home that you purchased from Seller A,
  to Buyer B, for $150,000.
- On the day of closing, Buyer B will bring to closing, $150,000, to buy the house.
- The title company/attorney will then use the $150,000 from Buyer B to pay off Seller A's amount of $100,000.
- The difference of $50,000 (minus any miscellaneous expenses) goes to you, the investor, as profit.

2. Secondly, you can wholesale even though you used your own money to purchase and close on the property. When this happens, you can turn around and sell it to an investor or a rehabber. The difference between the selling price and the buying price will be your profit.

3. Thirdly, you can use the exit strategy known as *assignment*. What this means is that you have the right to assign the contract that you signed with the homeowner/seller, to

another fellow investor or another interested party, for a fee. In this case, it would be appropriate to communicate your intention to the seller. Your profit will be the assignment fee.

Wholesaling is beneficial to new investors who want to raise cash quickly. It is worth noting that this strategy does not require the use of your own money or credit to get the deal done. All you are doing at this point is putting the property in contract with contingencies, which allows you ample time to wholesale properties to investors or to someone that may be interested in rehabbing the property if it needs repairs.

One caution that I will give you is that you need to factor in the profit that you expect out of the deal, before you close or sign any contract to seal up the deal. Being greedy is effortless. You need to guard against that, especially if the property requires a lot of repairs. When wholesaling the property to someone, that buyer may also have expectations of making some substantial profit from the deal as well. Be sure to leave some serious money on the table for your buyer. Also, be sure to factor in your profit so that you don't end up disappointed.

To stress this point, let's say that you found a house that is valued at $100,000, after all repairs have been completed. Secondly, let's say that the property needs about $10,000 in repairs. If your formula is to purchase a property at $0.60 on the dollar, you will then place your newly found property in a contract for $60,000. You will then make sure that you have a contingency in the deal to close in about 60 days. As soon as you sign the contract with the seller, place an advertisement in the newspaper, or on craigslist, in a classified page, or somewhere in a weekend shopper. The ad should read as follows: "Motivated, Desperate Seller. Cheap. Cash. Call Now." If you place an ad like this, be prepared, because your phone is about to ring off the hook. That is to say that you are bound to get many calls.

Before you place the advertisement in the paper, be sure that you know exactly what you will be selling the property for. Once a call comes in, and you agree with the price offered, the next thing to do, without any delay, is to meet and sign the contract with your new buyer. In this case, you become the seller. Be sure to fax the purchase contract to buy the house for $60,000, and your sales contract to your title company. The title company will do all the paperwork for you and close on the property. You don't have to be there. The next thing for you to do is to drive by and pick up the check for the difference of $20,000, which is your profit, in this example. Remember: to make a good profit on such a strategy, you need to find a good deal. If it is not a good deal, you may not be able to sell it, and you may end up getting stuck with it.

LEASE OPTION

Lease option is another strategy that you can use to make offers on properties without spending your own money or placing your credit on the line. In this case, you lease the property from a motivated seller, for a set amount and for a specified time. The longer you lease the property, the better (probably between 1 to 15 years).

This is what you do. Lease the property at the lowest rent possible, with an option to purchase the property below market value. This will give you the right or the option to buy the property.

One thing that I like about lease option is that you don't have to exercise your option. You are not obligated to purchase it. Should conditions in the market change, you can either exercise your option to buy it and make lots of money, or you can easily walk away from it. That is why we call it an option. One thing that you may want to remember, though, is that in some situations you may end up losing whatever deposit you may have placed on the property, if that was a requirement before signing the contract.

An example: Let's say that you lease a property from the owner, with an option for about $800 a month. Let's also assume that you then turn around and lease the same property to someone else, for $1,200 a month. Your monthly profit from this example will be $400 until you exercise your option. So, if your option price to buy the property is $200,000, with a value of $245,000, at any given time, you can sell the property to somebody for about $230,000 to $245,000, thus creating a profit of at least $30,000.

Now that you know how to analyze and evaluate deals, hurry very quickly, without any hesitation, to Chapter 5. Yes, Chapter 5, where we will discuss *proven ways to negotiate and buy properties*. We will also consider when you should walk away from a deal. Go; go there now!!!

Chapter 5

Proven Ways to Negotiate and Buy Properties

"Let every eye negotiate for itself and trust no agent."
–William Shakespeare
"Let us never negotiate out of fear.
But let us never fear to negotiate."
–John F. Kennedy

WHEN TO BUY AND WHEN TO WALK AWAY

Negotiating is an art that must not be ignored in the real estate industry. It requires the quickness of mind and the determination to achieve the results that you set out to accomplish. What is it that you are looking for? Who can you count on to help you in attaining your goal? Is it a real estate agent? An acquisition manager that you hired to find properties for you? A bird dog, or other real estate investors?

The ability to differentiate a good deal from a bad deal is essential when you get to the phase of negotiations. One of the things that plague real estate investors is not knowing when to buy or when to walk away from a deal. It is also crucial to know what your exit strategy is before you consider making an offer on a property.

When Do You Buy?

As I discussed in Chapter 4, you buy the property after you have considered your exit strategy and have defined your buying criteria. In other words, what exactly do you want to make on a wholesale deal? Is it $10,000? Or do you want quick cash of $2,000? Do you want to make about $25,000 out of the deal, or do you want more money from it?

Once you have decided on your profit margin, concentrate on the vital aspects that could impact your return on investment (ROI). The questions to ask yourself are as follows: "How much money and time do I want to invest in this property to enable me to achieve my targeted profit?" To answer this question, let us look at the *money factor.*

To invest in a property, you need to decide on your initial investment, or the amount of money that you are willing to put into the property. How many repairs are you ready to make? How extensive do you want the repairs to be? Do you want to paint the entire house, or touch up on specific areas—kitchen, family room, bathroom, or hallway? How about the flooring? Do you want to leave what is currently there now, or do you want to change the wooden flooring to carpet? Do you want to dispose of the current countertop and install a new one? How do the cabinets and vanities look? What is your budget for the repairs? These are questions that you must answer. Once you have responded to these questions, you must then factor in the profit or the cash flow that you want to realize from the deal. You must then place the property in contract immediately.

When Do You Walk Away?

Now that we have discussed when to purchase your investment property, let us look at when it is appropriate to walk away from purchasing a property during the acquisition process. You should walk away when you realize that the house under consideration does not meet your defined buying criteria. This could be because the price of the property is too high, and the seller is refusing to negotiate with you to drop the price to meet your buying criteria. Or it could be that the repairs are too much for you to handle. It could also be because the property could become a burden or a deterrent, and not fetch you the profit or cash flow that you are looking for. Should that happen, I will suggest that you move on and find another property immediately, and use the same yardstick, measurement, or checklist to see if the new house you want to purchase comes any closer to meeting your acid test.

I don't care how gorgeous or huge or lovely the house may appear to be. The problem is that if you go against your buying criteria, you may end up in trouble and not realize what you initially set out to accomplish, which is making the profit or the cash flow that you desire. This is why it is imperative not to fall in love with the property. Treat it strictly like a business.

One of the tragedies that I have seen with new investors is that they tend to fall in love with the property very quickly. I will never forget walking into a beautiful house in Los Angeles, with a new investor, to look at the property and then determine if it met her buying criteria. As soon as the real estate agent opened the door, and she saw the family room and the living room, she could not hold herself back. She yelled out, "Look at this beautiful kitchen; look at the gorgeous bathroom. Oh, my God, the appliances are just off the chart!" All business immediately went out of the window for her, and she instantly became emotional. I had to look at her and remind her as to why we were there. Our agenda was to look at that property, analyze it, and then decide if it met our buying criteria, not to fall in love with the property.

It took me quite a while to get this education across to her because, even though she had her own house, which was somewhat smaller than what we were looking at, she could not resist the temptation of seeing herself in that house, not as an investor but as a homeowner. All that she could see was herself living in that house. This is what I want you to get out of your system when you are negotiating and analyzing properties to purchase for investment. If you begin to look at the carpet, the paint, or the tiles on the wall, from an emotional point of view, before you know it, you will have fallen in love with the property—as a dwelling place for you. You will become subjective with your negotiations and may end up buying the property, whether it makes good business sense or not. Be careful. This is business.

KNOW WHAT THE OTHER SIDE IS LOOKING FOR

It is equally important to know what the other hand [the seller] is looking for. This is important to you. Once you have that information, you will know exactly how to craft your offer. Through your negotiations, you should be able to tell if the seller is looking for money or if he or she is looking to offload the property. If the seller only wants to get rid of the property, then you have a motivated seller who is desperate and would be willing to negotiate with you no matter what. Your offer on this kind of deal could be *lease option*, *subject to*, or even a *cash offer*.

DO YOUR DUE DILIGENCE

Due diligence should not be taken for granted, especially when it comes to making an offer on a property. It would be prudent on your part to call the city and find out what businesses are coming into the area, and what companies are moving out.

Secondly, you may want to know whether the zoning is right on the property. You will be surprised, but the fact of the matter is that sometimes the city may have plans for the land on which the house is built. If you do not check with the city, you may wake up to a huge surprise: that the city is going to use the land for something that neither the seller, nor you, the buyer, anticipated. Once you have this information, my advice to you is to tread carefully so that you do not get yourself all tangled up in unnecessary problems.

Be positive and knowledgeable. Make your offers from a superior point of view. You can only do this after you've done your homework strategically, as well as intelligently. When the seller realizes that you know your craft, he will be eager to do business with you.

Be sure to have a winning attitude the first time you meet with the seller. Do not just walk in blindly, thinking that the house is going to be offered to you on a silver platter. You must be confident in yourself. The way to become confident in yourself is what we discussed above: doing your due diligence, quantifying your numbers and standing by your numbers, and making sure that you are not just there to steal the house but are making it a win-win situation for both you and the seller.

MEETING WITH YOUR REAL ESTATE AGENT

Before you meet with your real estate agent regarding a property that you are interested in buying, make sure that you know exactly how much you are willing to pay for the investment property. The worst mistake you can ever make is to be all over the board without having a figure in mind before your meeting. I should tell you that this is critical information that you must have. Do not allow FEAR of losing the property to dominate your thinking process and, thereby, paying market value for it. If your offer is too high, but the real estate agent has your interests at heart, she would do whatever it takes to make sure you buy below market price. Consider your realtor as a co-worker who wants you to succeed. Do not be intimidated to let her know where you stand when it comes to price negotiations. Your success is her success as well. So be open in your dealings with your realtor.

If you are not comfortable with any suggestions that she comes up with, let her know that you will get back to her later. This would give you the chance to analyze the deal further, and discuss it with your team, spouse, or someone more experienced than yourself. Do not allow yourself to be drawn into what is known as *paralysis of analysis*. That is over-analyzing a deal till you lose it. Real estate requires speed, so my advice is that you make a swift decision and get back to the realtor with an answer. Otherwise, you may end up losing the deal, especially if it is a good one, due to your indecision.

THE RESEARCH PHASE

Before you make an offer on a property, be sure to do your homework. You must know how much the property is worth. See if there are different ways to create or force equity once you purchase it. In other words, what are other ways to add value to the property, so that its value will be as high as you want it, to enable you to get the profit that you want out of it? To accomplish this, you may need systems that you can use to do a comparative market analysis on the property. Your realtor can provide you with COMPS. If you do not have a realtor, there are other systems that you could subscribe to that would give you similar results. Although I work with realtors very carefully, I also have access to Haines Criss-Cross systems, which I use personally to run the numbers very quickly before I meet with my real estate agent.

BE CAREFUL ABOUT WHAT YOU SAY

Talking too much during negotiations can cause you to lose a lot of money. When I started as a new investor, one of the lessons that my mentor taught me was to *shut up* when it comes to negotiations. He said, "Do not be the first person to make the offer. He called it *diarrhea of the mouth*. He said to let the other party open his or her mouth first, because whoever opens their mouth first, loses. His advice has served me well in all my negotiations. It was very uncomfortable at first. But now it is easy. Not being the first to mention the amount of the offer, gives you room for maneuverability. You can easily find a middle ground to negotiate. This is a huge problem for new or inexperienced investors. They think that by opening their mouth, talking, talking, and talking, they will prove to the other party that they know what they are talking about. Instead, the seller looks at them and realizes that they can easily be taken. Fewer words go a long way, and put more money in your pocket.

Secondly, when you are careful with your words and do not open your mouth to make the first offer, the other party often becomes nervous, and will spill out the amount that he or she wants. So, if I am negotiating on an electrical job that would cost only $200, but I open my mouth first by letting my electrician know that I have only $300 to work with, guess what he is going to charge me? Of course, $300. But if I ask what he would charge me, and then remain silent, he would be forced to open his mouth, and would probably charge me only $150 or $200.

I have used this strategy in several negotiations, and it has worked for me most of the time. I remember my transmission going out entirely, on one of my older vehicles. I took it to a transmission shop first, for a free estimate. They told me outright that it would cost me $4,000 to rebuild it. Because I know that my mechanic could do the job, I took the vehicle to him to repair the transmission. What you must realize is that before I took my vehicle to my mechanic, I had already done my homework. When I asked my mechanic how much he was going to charge me for the transmission, I did not divulge to him the price that the other transmission shop quoted me. I just asked him a question and then kept my mouth shut. For about five minutes, we both stood there staring at each other. I knew that he wanted me to open my mouth and tell him how much money I had to work with. But I refused to open my big mouth. He eventually opened his mouth and said to me that he was going to charge me $1,800 to rebuild the transmission, with one-year warranty. I then started to negotiate the amount down, not only on the price of the transmission but also on the warranty. By the time I was done with him, he had reduced the cost of the transmission to $1,600, with a two-year warranty.

Now, look at this scenario: if I had opened my mouth first, by telling him what the other shop was going to charge me for the same work he was going to do for me, I would have easily lost

$2400, just because I opened my big mouth. My advice to you is the same advice that my mentor gave me. Shut up, and do not have *diarrhea of the mouth*, and you will do well. This leads us to my next point.

THE PREGNANT PAUSE TECHNIQUE

This technique is a compelling strategy that you can adopt during negotiations. You can use it when the most talkative client cannot stand the silence in the conversation any longer, and begins to provide or divulge more information. So, let's say that during an intense negotiation, I become immediately silent. However, my client, or the other negotiator, is not satisfied with the offer that I had just placed on the table. Because I remain silent and stare at him expectantly, he will begin to either drop the price to keep the conversation going, or he will give me more information about the deal, which I could in turn use to negotiate a better outcome. This strategy is known as *the pregnant pause*.

What you need to realize is the fact that there are clients and sellers, or even buyers, out there who cannot tolerate long pauses or long silences in conversations. They just can't shut up, and will keep talking. They will continue to talk until they tell you everything that you need to know, because the long silence kills them. They cannot stand the fact that you are staring at them without saying anything. Whenever you come across someone like that during negotiations, adopt this technique, and watch what happens. You will receive essential and valuable information that you could use to your advantage, if you force yourself to be quiet and not say a word.

DO NOT BE LAZY

This phase of the *negotiation strategy* is just as critical. Gather as much information as you can on the seller, as well as on the property and the neighborhood. If you want to depend solely on what your real estate agent tells you, you may end up leaving plenty of money on the table, which could easily have been yours, had you taken the time to gather the necessary information. Do not be lazy by outsourcing this to someone else. Remember, information is power. The more information you have, the better. This is where a lot of newbies or inexperienced investors fail big. Once you have good information, you will walk away with a better outcome, just because you have enough knowledge about the property, the seller, the situation, the neighborhood, etc. This gives you room to negotiate better, and to counter anything that the other party may bring your way.

The reason why you want more information about the seller is to find out exactly what she wants. You may assume that all the seller may need is just a lot of money, and therefore, you may do just that. But experience has taught me that this is not always the case. Sometimes all the seller needs is for someone to take the property over immediately, so she can move on with life. Motivated sellers have different issues that are pressing on them to sell the house as soon as possible. In such a situation, having a terrific conversation with the seller, to find out what she wants, is vital. What if all she wants is a moving amount of $3,000? But you did not have that conversation with her. Instead, you are banging your head against the wall as to where to find $88,000 to close on the house. That could be a recipe for disaster, because the first person that may end up offering her what she needs—in this case, the $3,000—would be the one that she would give the deed of the house to. Be nice, and have the necessary conversation with the house owner, because she would look at you as the one and only person that helped to solve her problem when she was in distress.

LISTENING TO THE SELLER IS KEY

Active listening during this phase of negotiation should not be taken lightly. What you must realize is that there is a difference between active listening and passive listening. Whenever you are talking to a motivated seller, do not come across as one that sits there and absorbs information without full engagement with the seller, as though you are not interested in what the seller has to say. Something must have pushed that individual to become motivated. It could be financial difficulties or probate issues, which she would not like to continue to deal with. It could be due to a horrible divorce that has forced her to become a motivated seller.

You, as the investor, are the one that she would look up to, to help solve whatever problem she might be faced with. I touched on this lightly in the above paragraph. What you don't want the seller to do is to label you as one who wants to steal her house.

How could she jump to such a conclusion? It comes out loud and clear when you seem not to care, and you show her how preoccupied you are. An example of this is when you are not looking her directly in the eye, and you are going through a pile of papers when she is seriously divulging information to you. In her mind, you do not care about her, and you are not acknowledging what is being said to you. By all means, do not disrespect her by allowing yourself to be distracted by other trivial things. You will easily miss valuable information that she may want you to grab. To avoid these issues, concentrate on her, and her only.

Also, feel free to get involved verbally by repeating her words back to her. For example, you may hear the seller say the following: "I want to move out no later than July 30th." Your response back to her would be: "Are you saying that you would not do the deal should we close on August 2nd, as opposed to July 30th?" An exchange like this will create or form a bond between the two of you. The homeowner may not hold back any information from you. She would realize that you are a great person to deal with. Why? Because you listened to her and gave her your undivided attention.

MAKE HER FEEL GOOD

I will never forget the disappointment on her face when she saw me at the gym, and with this colossal disappointment written all over her face, she blurted out the following words: "Oh, I just gave my house away for nothing." I was wondering what she was talking about and why she was so disappointed. She then began to tell me how she received an offer on her house, which was listed for $450,000.

"So, what happened?" I inquired.

"I received an offer for $380,000, to which I countered with $400,000. I was hoping that she would walk away and not take it. But to my surprise, she immediately accepted my counter-offer, and she is closing on my house in two weeks. I feel like a fool. I should have countered it for $430,000."

"So, why didn't you?" I asked.

To which she responded, "I was afraid of losing the buyer."

I gave you this example so you will realize that this kind of negotiation does happen. But negotiations that end up with you giving in very quickly, are not always good ones. Sometimes it is good to go back and forth; otherwise, you will feel cheated and will think that you got a terrible deal. This happens, especially when the seller or the client that you are dealing with accepts your offer without any considerable resistance.

Make sure that you introduce some resistance in the dialogue of negotiations. I was taught by my mentor to always ask the following question: "Is that the best you can do?" I cannot begin to tell you how powerful this statement is, and how it has served me well over the years, and in diverse situations. Whether making an offer on a house, a car, or having a contractor work on something for me, or even the cleaning lady, I always ask: "Is that the best you can do?" Once I ask that, I shut my mouth and, almost every time, they come back with a better deal for me. To them, they feel good that they got me at exactly where they wanted me, and they feel as if they have earned an excellent deal.

ASK FOR CONCESSIONS

Be careful not to give away something without asking for anything in return. Even if you are giving your clients what they want, be sure always to get something in return. It is a tit-for-tat game that you must master. So, how do you go about something like this? It is better handled, on most occasions, with a question: "If I were to pay you cash, and close in 14 days, would you be willing to then drop your price from $60,000 to $50,000? Would you agree that this is a fair exchange?"

When you ask a question, the chances are that the seller will take the opportunity to tell you exactly what they think a fair exchange is for what you are asking. At which point, you can also negotiate up or down from your initial position. If, on the other hand, you stand your ground by stating what you are looking for, you will be tied up, thereby limiting yourself to possible concessions that may result in a better deal for you.

When it comes to concessions, be sure to concede gradually, bit by bit.

Creating Wealth

Let's look at an example:

Buyer B makes an initial offer of $200,000, on a pretty house with an asking price of $250,000. Seller A then counters back at $240,000; so Buyer B was forced to up his offer to $220,000, at which point Seller A counters back at $230,000, which forces Buyer B to counter back at $235,000.

So, instead of what happened in the example above, what if you punch holes in your offer, or in Buyer B's offer, by looking for items that would force the hand of Seller A to concede and drop the price drastically. So, Buyer B initially offers $200,000, at which point Seller A counters back at $240,000 on the asking price of $250,000. At this point, Buyer B, instead, begins to punch holes in the counter offer from Seller A, by dwelling on repairs that the house seriously needs once he purchases the house, and thereby convinces Seller A. At this point, Buyer B counters at $205,000, based on the list of repairs that need to be made. Seller A, in turn, counters back at $230,000. Instead of taking the bait and following up with a counter, Buyer B diverts the conversation and dwells on other benefits, such as paying off the mortgage so that Seller A would not have to deal with it any longer; thereby giving him peace of mind. At this point, Buyer B ups his offer by adding $5,000 more to his offer of $205,000, bringing it to $210,000. Since the benefits enumerated by Buyer B sounds excellent to Seller A, he drops his asking price to $225,000. At this point, Buyer B lets Seller A know that they would have a deal if Seller A would accept $215,000; and they strike a deal.

As you can see from the second example, Buyer B walks away with a difference of $35,000 ($250,000-$215,000) as opposed to only $15,000 ($250,000-$235,000) from the first example. Just look at the vast difference of a whopping $20,000 that you could use to put down on another property, or for a vacation.

KEEP YOUR EXCITEMENT TO A MINIMUM

On most occasions, a lot of sellers think that their house is the only one that you are considering, and that you would be stuck if they did not give in to your demands. They then begin to play hardball. Whenever you realize this, be sure to let the seller know that there are other houses that you are considering making offers on. The best way to go about this is through conversations with the seller. Set up a time to view their house. During your discussion with the owner, let the discussion go as follows: "I would like to come and see your house at 4:30 pm, but I may be somewhat late, probably about 20 minutes, since I will be stopping to look at three other houses that I am considering as well." Refrain from the temptation of letting the seller know how much interest you have in his/her house. I don't care how lovely the house is. Be careful not to give too many compliments about the house, even if it is priced low, or if the neighborhood is the best that you want to invest in. Keep your excitement to yourself until you secure it and close on it.

PRESENTING LOW OFFERS

In this profession, I have gone through quite a few real estate agents. The reason is that a lot of realtors do not like when my offers are lower than what they expect them to be. So, to help substantiate my offers, I always point out problem areas in the house. You will have to find flaws that you can point out to real estate agents, or to the seller that you are dealing with. Make sure that you write those problem areas down so that you do not forget. It is beneficial if you can verbalize some of those repairs to the seller or the listing real estate agent. Remember to be as objective as you can. Do not make the seller or the agent think that you are being personal. Let them know that you are there to make a profit, and that your investment in the house has to make sense and be a win-win situation for both of you. Communicate your willingness to walk away if they are not willing to accept your offer. It would be beneficial to let them know that you could easily part as friends, without any hard feelings, should the deal go south.

ASK QUESTIONS

Although I hinted on this before, I feel it is necessary to mention it again. Asking a lot of questions during negotiations can give you lots of answers, clues, and insights into what your seller is thinking. You want to know what is motivating him to get rid of his property. Some of the questions that I have used in the past, and I continue to apply even today, are as follows:

- How long have you owned this property?
- How much do you owe on it?
- Why exactly do you want to sell?
- What significant improvements have you made in the last three years?
- Why did you make those repairs?
- How much do you need if I were to pay you all cash today?
- How soon do you have to move out?
- What one thing would you like to change about the property if you had the chance?

As you can see from the questions above, it would serve you well if you use these tactics before and during negotiations. Again, your goal is to pull out the necessary information from your seller to understand what is driving them to sell the house. Once you understand this, you will find ways to meet that need. If you can get to the core of their motivation, through your questions, I would say that you will have accomplished almost 80% of your goal.

As an example, let's say that you came across an independent lady who just got married to an independent guy. Both of them have good jobs and owned homes before their marriage. As you can see, from this example, they need to get rid of one of the houses, since they do not want to continue to pay the mortgage on both of them. How would you get this information if they did not readily divulge it to you? There is no way for you to find out. Because you now have this information, you know precisely how to meet this core motivation. You can now put them at ease, and assure them that you will offload the burden of the mortgage from their shoulders, so that they are no longer saddled with the extra mortgage payment. You can, at this point, negotiate points that are important to you. It will enable you to harvest the results that you want.

If you do not ask questions to find out the actual reason why they want to get rid of the house, there is no way that you could satisfy their need. This is why it is so important to not only ask questions but also to listen very attentively, to enable you to get the deal and close on it. When you look, you get a better understanding, and you can ask more specific questions and clarifications.

DROP YOUR PRIDE

Whenever you are negotiating, especially for the price of a house, do not allow your pride to get in the way of achieving your goal. If the price is your primary concern, then be willing to compromise and make concessions in other areas. Make everything else as easy as possible. Do not go around telling people how great of a negotiator you are. Be very careful of your nonverbal cues, because some sellers can pick up on your pomposity easily. In many situations, what a seller needs is somebody who would be willing to hear them out, walk in their shoes, and empathize with whatever situations that they happen to be dealing with. If you do not show sympathy but go around bragging about yourself, you may end up losing the deal.

BE WILLING TO COMPROMISE

Compromising in situations, where you realize that the deal is about to go south, is not a bad thing at all. You need to know when to be firm and when to be flexible. This is very important during negotiations of a real estate deal. I'm not advocating that you should not be firm. It is crucial to stand your ground so you can achieve what you want out of the deal. Being firm also shows your seriousness about your business, and your assertiveness to be successful in this industry. But on the other hand, if you are not flexible at all, and will not move an inch from your position, chances are that you would end up killing the whole deal.

An example is that if your seller is willing to agree to most of your offers and stipulations that you deem important, please do not waste precious time sweating over little items. Rather, find a compromising ground as fast as possible, so that your seller would also feel good about the deal. If you do not want to compromise, you will end up leaving a bad taste in the seller's mouth. He would not trust you any longer if you should approach him about the same deal a month from now, should you change your mind. Remember that it is essential that the seller feels good, and recognize that the transaction is a win-win situation for everyone.

Negotiating real estate deals is never an easy thing, but at the same time, you should be willing to go the extra mile. Applying a little common sense during your negotiations would leave room for you in the long run. You would not only walk away happy but will end up with more deals based on referrals that your seller may bring to you. BE NICE, NOT A JERK!

Chapter 6

Proven Ways to Acquire Properties

Creativity is just connecting things. When you ask creative people how they did something, they feel a little guilty because they didn't really do it; they just saw something. It seemed obvious to them after a while. That's because t hey were able to connect experiences they've had and synthesize new things."
– **Steve Jobs**

Whereas the usual norm to acquiring properties is through financing with banks or purchasing with cash, it is crucial for you, as an investor, to realize that there are several other creative ways to buy or invest in properties, which do not always involve the use of cash or credit. I call these options the *creative ways* to acquire properties. I have used several of these strategies to buy my properties, aside from the use of cash and credit.

The more you master these strategies, the better off you will be in your negotiations with sellers. Having an excellent credit score is good. It is equally wonderful to have a lot of cash on hand that you can use to acquire properties. But before you resort to using your money or credit, let us explore the different creative ways that you can employ to accomplish the same goal. Once you know the various and several ways to invest in properties quickly, you will not be stuck with only one way of doing things but come up with different options that would be pleasing to both you and the seller.

STRATEGY 1: LEASE WITH AN OPTION TO PURCHASE

Before I explain what a *lease with an option to purchase* is, you need to first and foremost understand what a contract is.

So, what is a contract?

A contract is an agreement between two or more people. It could involve businesses, entities, organizations, or individuals. It permits the involved parties to either perform or put an end to performing an agreed-upon task. Usually, both parties receive something of value in exchange of what is agreed upon.

What constitutes a real estate contract?

In real estate, several elements must happen for a contract to take place.

There must be an offer and acceptance. Whenever someone is interested in purchasing a property, there must be an offer from one party to another party. In this example, let us say an offer from a buyer to a seller. The offer presented by the buyer must either be accepted or rejected by the seller once the offer is made. The offer and acceptance must both be in writing and must be signed by both individuals for it to a binding contract. In most cases, there is a limited amount of time given for the offer to either be accepted, countered, or rejected by the seller. If the time given expires without the offer being accepted or signed and returned to the buyer, it would be assumed that the seller does not like the offer, at which point the contract becomes null and void. At this juncture, neither party would be held liable for a breach of contract.

Counter-Offer

If, on the other hand, the seller wants to come up with what is known as a counter-offer, then the new offer has to be stated in writing and presented to the buyer. This takes place when there is something in the offer from the buyer (price, repairs, etc.) that may not be pleasing to the seller. Upon receipt of the counter-offer, it is up to the buyer at that point to either accept or reject the counter-offer from the seller. If the buyer agrees to the counter-offer (new offer), then the original contract will no longer be binding, and it must be modified to the new terms stated in the counter-offer, and must be executed based on the agreed upon terms.

The contract must have the following items:

1. Sale price of the property
2. Full name(s) of the seller

3. Full name(s) of the buyer
4. The legal address of the property
5. The terms of the contract
6. The expiration date of the contract

Lease Options

Now that you understand what a contract is, let us look at *lease with an option to purchase*. As explained above, one of the creative ways of investing or acquiring properties can be through the use of a *lease purchase*. Some refer to this creative way as *lease option, rent-to-own*, or *lease purchase*. It is a short form for what is commonly known as *lease with an option to purchase*. It is a strategy that combines a separate LEASE contract with an OPTION contract to purchase a property. Together, both form what is known as a *lease with an option to purchase or buy*. You could use this method to acquire either residential or commercial property.

Putting it all together for you to understand in simple terms, a lease option is where the seller allows you, the future interested buyer, or investor in this case, to rent or lease the house from the seller for a period of time before you exercise your option or purchase the house. Normally, this method of acquiring a property requires an option fee that cannot be refunded. It requires the seller to agree on the sale price and other miscellaneous terms. Both you and the seller have to come to terms on the deal through the signing of all paperwork covering the lease with an option to purchase.

What is an Option Contract?

An option contract is when you, an investor, or a buyer, promises the seller to buy the property but close at a later date. Sometimes the term of acquisition can be between one to three years, or whatever timeframe that is stated in the contract. The option contract protects you, the buyer, investor, or the individual making the offer, from the seller revoking the contract without performing.

One crucial thing that you must understand is the fact that you, as the buyer, have the option to purchase the home. What exactly does this mean? It means that you may or may not purchase the house, even though you have the option to buy it. Even though you have been given the exclusive right to purchase, you are not obligated to buy the home at the end of the term of the contract. The seller, on the other hand, is required to sell the house to you, should you choose to buy. However, should you decide to walk away from purchasing the property at the end of the agreed upon option contract, the seller is not obligated to return your option fee. The seller gets to keep the option fee. This is the only recourse that the seller has at this point.

In case you decide to purchase the property during the term agreed upon, or before the option expires, the option fee, on most occasions, would be applied towards the purchase price of the house, or could be used as a down payment.

So, let us go over everything mentioned above. A lease option transaction is between you, the investor, tenant, or buyer (optionee), and the seller (optionor). It involves contracts (explained above), which include the following:

1. Option Contract:
    a. Timeframe of the option contract
    b. Option fee

2. Rental Agreement:
    a. Terms of the rental
    b. Monthly rental payments
    c. Timeframe of the lease
    d. Deposit amount (to mention a few)

How Does All This Work for the Investor?

Once you have found a property that interests you, and the owner is willing to sell it to you through the strategy of a *lease option*, you would sign a *lease option agreement* with the seller, or the *optionor*. You must be willing to negotiate with the seller at this point, by requesting the most extended term possible, and also the lowest rent. The goal is for you, the investor, to sublet the house to a tenant of interest. Structure the deal in such a way that the rent that you receive from subletting the house would be as high as possible, to enable you to make enough money to cover the rent that you pay to your seller. If you don't structure the deal well, you may end up losing money and not being in the position to pay the rent as spelled out in your agreement, so you can have enough money left for you. The difference between what you collect and what your payout will be, is your cash flow. The difference then becomes your profit from the deal. Before this deal takes place, it would be a good idea for you to let the landlord know your intentions, so that he or she is not surprised when he finds out that you have sublet the property to someone else.

Let's look at an example:

Let's say that you received a call from a motivated seller—Sally—who has to sell her house, which is worth $200,000, because she is being transferred to another state. The house, as we know it, is in good condition. The balance on the loan is $144,000, with a monthly payment of $1,420. She does not want to list her house with a real estate agent, since she does not want to pay any commission. What she is asking for, though, is $180,000. The loan is assumable, should someone be interested. Fortunately, for Sally, an investor, by the name of Ben, heard about this house and rushed to see her. Upon learning what Sally was requesting, rather than Investor Ben assuming the loan or going to the bank to obtain a loan to purchase the house, he suggests entering into a lease with an option to purchase contract, which was wholehearted agreed to by Sally. Buyer Ben then offers to buy the house for $170,000, with a three-year term and the right to renew for a 4th year if need be. Seller Sally agrees, and Investor Ben gives her an option fee of $2,000, and the loan to be paid off at the time of sale, for $144,000.

At this point, Investor Ben, who has been keeping a buyer's list, called on one of his potential clients. He offered Mr. Brown a lease with an option to purchase Sally's house. He gave Mr. Brown a sales price of $210,000, with a two-year term, a monthly rent payment of $1,990, and a non-refundable option fee of $10,000, with no option to renew. A renewal of the option would cost Mr. Brown $5,000 for one year's extension. The amount due at closing from Mr. Brown would be $200,000.

Let us look at the numbers:

Seller Sally:
Asking Price	$180,000
Loan Balance	$144,000
Cash	$ 36,000

Investor Ben's Offer:
Lease Option (3-year term)	$170,000
Option Fee	$ 2,000
Cash Due to Sally at Closing	$ 24,000
Loan to be paid off	$144,000

Investor Ben's Lease Options to Buyer Brown:
Sales Price	$210,000
Non-refundable option fee	$ 10,000
Amount Due at Closing	$200,000
Monthly Rent	$ 1,990

Investor Ben's Final Net Profit

Profit on Option Fee from Buyer Brown, minus $2,000 to Sally)	$ 8,000 ($10,000
Monthly Cash Flow rent received: $1,990 minus $1,420 payout)	$ 570 (Monthly
Income from Sale at Closing minus $168,000 to Sally, minus $10,000 received from Brown)	$ 32,000 ($210,000

As you can see from the above example, the total amount of profit made, just from one deal using this strategy, is $40,570. I think you can be happy to employ this formula, and do it over and over again with various properties. In the several years that I have been investing, I have taught several students this strategy, and they have used it over and over again. As far as I know, some of my students have only used this strategy, to their advantage.

Thus, this strategy offers several advantages, which I want to spell out. From the above example, the following are benefits to Sally:

1. Had debt relief
2. Did not have to do any repairs
3. No property management fee from out of pocket

4. Continued to receive tax benefits until the house was out of her name or sold
5. Preserved her credit, since Investor Ben did not default the monthly payment
6. Received a lump-sum of cash at closing
7. Avoided due on sale clause
8. Retained ownership until the house sold

Advantages to Investor Ben are as follows:

1. Received the substantial amount of non-refundable fee
2. Did not have any risk for non-payment
3. Received monthly cash flow
4. Received cash at closing
5. No advertising fee, since Brown is already occupying the property
6. Did not have to use his credit
7. Had no repairs to worry about (Buyer Brown paid for all repairs)
8. Did not incur any holding costs or realtor commissions
9. Little money down for an option fee
10. Dealt only with a qualified buyer (Brown)

Advantages to Buyer Brown:

1. Able to occupy the property immediately
2. Regarded the property as his own house
3. Had enough time to pay down payments on an installment basis

4. Had ample time to raise credit score to get a reasonable rate on his mortgage

STRATEGY 2: SHORT SALES

During the market crash in 2007, we saw the influx of foreclosures in this nation as we had never seen before. The foreclosures were so bad that in almost every community that you went to, you saw a For Sale sign. The next strategy that we are going to discuss is *short sale*.

What Is a Short Sale?

A short sale is when a bank or a lender decides to take less amount on a property than what is owed on the mortgage of the same property. This is because the balance of the mortgage on the property is higher than the actual value of the said property. Even though the bank agrees to take a lesser amount for the loan, on many occasions, the lender or bank may or may not forgive the remaining difference after the agreed amount is paid. In the event that they don't forgive the difference, which is also known as a deficiency, the borrower is forced to pay it one way or another.

How Does Short Sale Occur?

A short sale happens when the borrower defaults on the loan, or is unable to make the monthly mortgage payments as agreed to at the time of purchasing the house. As soon as the borrower misses the first payment, the bank would immediately start calling the customer to make sure payments are made. If the borrower is unable to make payments for up to three to four months, the house is placed in foreclosure.

However, if the borrower reaches out to the bank and requests a short-sale, and it is accepted, the property will not be foreclosed on.

The question is why any bank or lender would agree to a discounted payoff on a loan, whereas they could get a full payback on the outstanding mortgage. One thing that you need to understand is that sometimes a property may have several lenders associated with that one property, with different lien holding positions. It is possible that any lender in a 2nd, 3rd, or 4th position could lose all their money, should the property go into foreclosure and be sold on the auction block. Also, foreclosures are generally costly and time-consuming. These properties add risk to the lender in junior positions.

If the house goes all the way into foreclosure, and the bank gets the house back, there are several liabilities and ongoing costs that the lender would have to incur. Some of the costs are as follows: maintenance, utilities, insurance, taxes, realtor commissions, vandalism (if the property is in a dangerous area), theft of copper pipes, appliances, etc. With all these eventualities, the banks or lenders would rather avoid all the unforeseen contingencies, and would instead opt for a short sale. In that event, the house could be liquidated quickly, thereby minimizing or removing all possibilities of future liabilities and losses completely.

Short Sale Process

There is no specific timeline that could be placed on the short sale process. It varies from lender to lender. Although all lenders would have the borrower believe that it would only take thirty days for a decision to be made, it goes way beyond that. The reason why it is such a painful exercise for the investor is because of the documents that have to be presented to the bank over and over again, because some lenders are notorious for not receiving your documents when you fax or mail them. I have had the experience where I submitted the same documents about four to five times, to the same fax number, before the bank acknowledged receipt.

Once you embark on this process, some of the documents that you will have to submit to the lender are as follows:

1. Hardship Letter(s)
2. Bank Statements
3. Tax Returns
4. Pay Stubs
5. Mortgage Statements
6. Lease Agreements
7. Home Owners Association Letters
8. Insurance Declaration Pages
9. Proof of Tax Payments

10. 4506-T
11. RMA or Request of Mortgage Assistance
12. Dodd-Frank Certification

After submission of the requested documents, you need to check with the bank occasionally to make sure that they are not missing any documents from you. Sometimes they will not reach out to you on time. By the time they inform you of missing documents, the time has already elapsed, causing you to restart the short sale process all over again.

Benefits to the Investor

Once the short sale is approved, the borrower is often released from liability for the deficiency, as I explained above, although this is not always the case. As you can see, short sales can be a gold mine for the real estate investor. You can invest in this kind of deal with no money from your pocket. If you need money badly to close, and don't want to lose the property, you can use transactional funding or private funds to close on the house. If you did your homework well, and negotiated successfully with the bank, you could end up with a substantial amount of equity in the property. This will give you the flexibility of either renting or selling the property quickly to interested parties, at a significant profit.

Example:
This is assuming that after a hard marketing campaign, you were able to find a property that is in foreclosure, with a value

of $250,000, with a defaulted first mortgage of $147,000, which requires an amount of $5,500 to cure the debt. Unfortunately, the property comes with estimated repairs of $20,000. Upon further research, you found other liens on the property as follows: a second mortgage of $89,000, with arrears of $6,500; and a third mortgage of $20,000, with a total outstanding amount of $1,400. The total liens on this property, at its current state, stands at $269,900.

As a good negotiator, you were able to cut down the second mortgage to a $5,000 cash payoff, and beat down the third lender to accept only $1,000. You then decided to cure the first amount of $5,500, bringing the purchase price to $100,500 ($89,000+$11,500), plus a total closing cost of $2,500, resulting in a total purchase price of $103,000.

The above negotiations gave you substantial equity in this property, with a handsome reward of $127,000 ($250,000-$100,500-$2,500) after repairs. You can use either private funds, transactional funds, or even hard money to purchase this property, without any problems at all. Although this strategy may take a long time, sometimes two to three months, before you get an answer from the lender, it is worth it. My recommendation to you is to sharpen your marketing and negotiating skills, and find homeowners with properties in foreclosure or with defaulted notes. Once you have a property like that, do not waste time at all. Present the required documents and follow the suggested steps to acquire the property. Be diligent and don't give up.

STREATEGY 3: EXPIRED LISTINGS

Another proven way that you can use to acquire properties is through advertising to expired listings. What exactly are expired listings? This happens when a seller gives the home to a real estate agent to sell on his behalf, in exchange for a commission after the house sells. On many occasions, the house stays on the market for the duration of the contract, and does not sell during the period of the contract.

This may be because the price is too high, or sometimes the house would not sell because of major repairs that the seller does not want to fix. Or better yet, it could be that the location of the property is not all that attractive to the market and, therefore, is not looked on favorably by interested buyers. When this happens, an expired listing occurs, and a motivated seller is created. At this point, the seller may be willing to reduce the asking price of the house.

So, the question is, how can you access a list of expired listings? This is where your real estate agent, or any realtor, comes in. The only system that houses these listings is the MLS system. Therefore, any realtor will be able to supply you with the list of houses or properties that have expired from the MLS system. Once you receive the list, it behooves you to generate a well-crafted, persuasive and convincing marketing letter to the owners of the houses with the expired listings. The letters that you mail out should produce calls from the motivated sellers who need you to solve their problem by purchasing their house.

The strategy is for you to mail to the expired listings, at least two times in a given month, with another follow-up letter to the same addresses or listings. If the letters do not yield the results that you are looking for, then it would be good to send either a yellow letter or postcard to the same addresses. Procrastination is an enemy to the real estate investor. My advice is for you to mail the letters as soon as the listing expires. Do not wait. Remember, they need you, because at this point, you are the only who could solve their ongoing problem for them.

Again, be sure to create a good relationship with a real estate agent who can supply you with the listings that have expired and have not been renewed. The way to convince the realtor to provide you with the list is to let them know that you will pay the finder's fee when you buy, and pay them a commission when the house sells.

STRATEGY 4: SUBJECT TO

A *Subject To* deal occurs when a homeowner issues the deed of the property to the buyer, without the buyer or investor paying off any of the liens that are associated with the property. In other words, a *Subject To* is when you acquire property *subject to* the underlying existing mortgage, along with all other liens or encumbrances that are attached to the property. This strategy grants you, the investor, immediate possession of the property. You can then turn around and rent it, wholesale it, or lease it with an option to buy, to an interested party.

Creating Wealth

This strategy is what I call a *sweet strategy*. You, the investor, do not assume the loan. You do not have to obtain hard money with ridiculous fees; you do not need transactional funding to close on the deal. All you do is take over the monthly payments that have already been set in place by the seller's lender.

As you can already envision, this strategy comes with several benefits:

1. You do not need to go to the bank for a mortgage.
2. You do not need to put your credit in jeopardy, since you do not need to have the deed issued to you.
3. The mortgage stays in the seller's name until you cash him/her out.
4. Your closing costs can be very minimal.
5. You can immediately start accumulating cash flow.
6. You can even sell the property and obtain an excellent net income.

As an investor, your credibility is on the line. The least mistake that you make can cost you substantially, whereby referrals that are supposed to come your way are halted. I am saying this because, once you take over a property *subject to*, you are obligated to make the payments on a timely basis. Remember, the seller trusted you to make those payments. Please make them, and do not cast a shadow on your name. The bible said: *"A good name is to be desired more than riches."* Preserve your good name, and do not muddy it. What you should be conscious about is to continue to make the payments so that the property does not slip into default.

What to Do After You Get the Deed

1. Complete a Purchase and Sale Agreement with the seller. Be sure to state in the contract that you have the flexibility to do due diligence.
2. The seller should authorize you to *Release Information to a Third Party*. Why? Because you need the authorization to discuss the mortgage with the lender. You also need authorization to order payoff amount, and also to find out about other delinquencies. You need authorization to transact any business that pertains to the loan.
3. Have a title company do a lien and title search on the property for you.
4. Check to see what and if there are repairs that need to be made.
5. Be sure to obtain a *Warranty Deed To Trustee*.
6. Place the property in a trust.
7. The trust owns the property, and the beneficiary owns the trust.
8. It would be good to obtain a *Limited Power of Attorney*, which would allow you to sign documents on the seller's behalf.
9. Be sure to have your attorney review all the documents, to be sure you stay within the confines of the law.

As you embark on this strategy, *Subject To*, be sure to clear out any misunderstandings with the seller. You are the problem solver that the seller is looking up to, to save her from her woes or doom. As sweet as this strategy may look, be sure not to overpromise what you cannot deliver. As you can agree, you do not need your cash to obtain a property *subject to*. If anything at all, you borrow funds if needed, to make repairs.

STRATEGY 5: WHOLESALING

The final strategy that I would like to discuss is what is known as *wholesaling*. It is the act of buying or tying up a property at a specified price, with the intention of selling the same property without doing any repairs (as-is) to the property, at a slightly higher price, for a quick profit.

Wholesaling happens when a real estate investor places a property in contract, and markets and sells the property to other real estate investors, or to a buyer's list or potential buyers. Once the property is in contract, the seller can assign the contract to a fellow investor or rehabber.

The purpose or goal of wholesaling is to make a quick profit, which is the difference between the amount contracted with your seller, and the price your buyer paid for unloading the property off your hands. This strategy calls for speed. This is because you want the contracted property to sell quickly, before the expiration of the contract with the original owner of the home.

Example:
Seller A placed a property in a contract for $70,000. The house, at this point, needs about $15,000 in repairs. The after-repair value shows that the house could sell for $130,000. Because Seller A is so desperate, and does not want to do the repairs herself, even though there is tremendous amount of money to be made after repairs, she instead decides to sell the property. Going through her buyer's list, she finds the telephone number of Investor Caitlin. Seller A then places a call to Investor Caitlin, and talks her into buying the property for $105,000. She then assigns the contract to Investor Caitlin, and Seller A makes a profit of $20,000, without owning the property.

Benefits of Wholesaling:

1. You can add contingencies to the contract.
2. You can back out of the deal if you cannot find a buyer, based on contingencies attached to the purchase contract
3. The risk to you is minimal, since you do not own the property.
4. Carrying costs to you can be zero.
5. Renovation costs to you are negligible, since you have not purchased the property.
6. You do not have to use your own money
7. You can save your credit, since it is not needed to transact a wholesale deal.
8. You can easily make a substantial amount of money from a quick sale or through a contract assignment.

Other strategies that you could look into are FSBO (for sale by owner) properties, bank notes, or real estate owned (REOs) properties, to mention a few.

Now that you are ready to purchase properties using the diverse strategies discussed above, quickly go to Chapter 7, where I will teach you proven ways to increase the value of properties.

Chapter 7

Proven Ways to Increase the Value of Your Property

"Now, one thing I tell everyone is learn about real estate. Repeat after me: real estate provides the highest returns, the greatest values and the least risk."
– **Armstrong Williams**

"Entrepreneurship is all about an idea that creates differentiated business value to one's customers. You must be able to convince your customers about the benefits that association with you or your products will give them. People are ready to pay if they are convinced about your services or products."
– **N. R. Narayana Murthy**

Rehabbing a property can be a daunting task. But when you put time, effort, and money into it, the benefits that you will reap can be substantial and beneficial. My first property was a run-down home at the time of purchase. Because I was so green and did not know what I was doing, I invested a tremendous amount of money and time into it, without realizing that I was fixing the house as if I was about to move into it myself. This is because I fell in love with the property, which is actually breaking one of the cardinal rules of real estate investing.

That is not what I am advocating here at all. On the other hand, I am not suggesting that you use inferior items for the rehab process. Rather, you need to use quality materials that would create WOW experiences when someone walks into your property. A potential client or buyer that walks into your house to view it should leave the premises with such satisfaction that would suggest that they would not want to look at any other property. If that happens, you have hit the jackpot.

When you don't cut corners but invest in materials that would put a smile on someone's face, you are sending a message to that potential client that you care about your customers.

The question then is, how do you achieve these successes in your rehabs, over and over again? Below are some suggestions that you may want to adhere to when rehabbing a property:

1. Before you buy, make sure that you have someone walk through the property. Have that individual make a list of all the items that need to be repaired. This person may either be your maintenance guy, an inspector, or a contractor.

2. Secondly, be sure to have the house inspected if at all possible. This will help you to know what you are getting yourself into before you close on the property. On the surface, everything may look good, but there may be some

hidden items that only inspection can reveal. So, take this advice seriously.

3. After you receive the list of items that need fixing, be sure to take care of them as quickly as possible and within reason. This will result in a massive reduction in repair expenses, thereby increasing the value to the property.

4. A lot of new investors like to hire a handyman, or someone that is pretty cheap. Sometimes that could be a good idea, but experience has taught me that using affordable handymen could be very costly. This is because, on many occasions, cheap handymen want quick cash, and do not necessarily know what they are doing. They will patch up items that they have not fixed. Hiring a person of such caliber will lead you to hire a more qualified person eventually, to undo what the cheap guy did. Unqualified handymen could cost you more time and money, and you end up losing potential clients. Be very careful not to allow yourself to be taken when it comes to hiring a contractor, handyman, or a repair person. Remember: some of the handymen are nothing but con men.

5. Before you begin rehabbing, get three different estimates before finalizing on the more qualified person that will do the work for you. Going through this process can be complicated and cumbersome. However, it will save you from the temptation of hiring the cheapest person that shows up first. Again, be sure that you are neither hiring the

most reasonable nor the most expensive person. Proceed cautiously.

6. Even though I do not want you to have a love fest with the property, be very careful that you do not fix the house anyhow you like, either. If you do, the house may stay vacant for a long period of time before you are able to rent or sell it. Fix the house in such a way that you will be happy with it, and your potential clients will not turn their backs on it but will chase you everywhere to buy it from you.

7. Depending on the kind of house that you buy, you may end up with either a lot of repairs or just some cosmetic items to be fixed. Whatever the case may be, be sure to have the work completed before you put your house on the market.

Having gone through some of the critical things that you need to do, let us look at how you can add substantial value to your property.

THE EXTERNAL

The outside of the house is the first thing that people see when they come to view your property. The exterior of the house determines whether they want to go in or leave. If the outside is not in good condition, that alone is enough to have them make a U-turn and not see the inside of your house. It must be inviting. It must be captivating. It must be attractive. Following are some suggestions that will help you to improve and add value to your house:

LANDSCAPING

Mow the Lawn

It is imperative that you mow the lawn. This should be a no-brainer—no argument about that. It should be done either once a week or at least every other week. Whether you mow the lawn or not, you are sending a message to your potential clients. Should you decide not to have your lawn look pretty, the message that you are sending out is that you do not care about your property, and that you do not care about those who may want to make this property their home. On the other hand, if you decide to cut the grass to an acceptable length, your property will look much more beautiful, and people would be drawn to it.

Mulch the Flower Beds

\If there are flowerbeds, make sure that you mulch them beautifully. Decide on the color of mulch that you want to use. I like black mulch, and that is what you will see around my properties. But sometimes, based on the color of the house, I may choose to go with the red color, because the house may have bricks on the outside. It is, however, your ultimate decision as to what color you want, and also the kind of texture that you would like to put in your flowerbeds.

Fertilize the Lawn

This is where a lot of new investors fail. They do not see the need in fertilizing the grass because it is not their primary residence. This is important because you don't want all sort of weeds overtaking your grass. Let the lawn look fresh, green, and lovely. Apply one to two applications of fertilizer. It will make your grass grow rich and look very inviting.

Sometimes your neighbors determine how nice your grass should look. This is because some of them do not care about landscaping and, therefore, end up having a horrible lawn. The competition in my neighborhood is fierce. No one will tell you to have a beautiful lawn. You will look ridiculous if your yard looks terrible. Whatever the situation may be, be sure to differentiate yourself from your neighbors.

TREES

If there are plenty of trees on your property, remove some of them. Use your discretion. Whatever trees you decide to keep, be sure to have them trimmed neatly. Whereas trees can beautify your house, sometimes they can cause you pain. They tend to develop long roots that can block your pipes, resulting in a lot of expenses for you. To avoid spending vast amounts of money in the future, hire a professional tree company to remove the huge trees from your lawn. The expense you will incur by removing the trees will be much less than leaving them to continue to grow, and thereby breaking or jamming your pipes.

GARAGE/CARPORT

One of the essentials that you may want to add, in case there is none on your property, is a carport or a garage. Should the house come with either an attached or detached garage, make sure that it is in perfect shape. Sometimes it would be beneficial for you to paint the garage. Have the inside cleaned out entirely, and let it be vacant for your potential tenant or buyer. New homeowners usually want an empty garage when they move in for the first time. This is because they typically like to leave some of their belongings in the garage for a period before moving such items inside the house. This gives them ample time to decide where they would want to place their belongings. You can imagine how they would feel if the garage is occupied with junk from the previous resident. Hire someone to clean out everything in the garage to free it up for the next client. In the case where there is no garage, you may want to consider investing in a carport, thereby adding value to your property.

POWER WASHING

Have your contractor or a professional person power wash the exterior of your house, before you apply paint, should you decide to paint the outside. Power washing the house will remove peeling paint, spiders and cobwebs, mold, mildew, and stains from leaves and sticks. It will make the house look fresh, and it will help maintain the value of the property. Also, power washing the house is a beautiful way to create a healthier environment for your clients or future buyers, and it will add value to your curb appeal and your property.

Should you be wondering what I mean by power washing, it is when you apply a high velocity of water pressure to your house, with the goal of cleaning it. A power washing machine can be purchased from Lowes, Home Depot, or any home maintenance/repair store. By using a power washing machine, you can apply more water pressure to clean the exterior of your house, through the hose that comes with the equipment at the time of purchase.

If you decide not to paint, it would still serve you well to power wash. As indicated above, it will keep your property looking great and fresh. Consider hiring a professional handyman, contractor, or someone who knows what they are doing, to pressure wash the house for you.

It will cut down on cost, and you would avoid the temptation of trying to save pennies and investing heavily in a piece of equipment that you do not know how to use. A professional, I assume, will be much cheaper in this case. Although I own a pressure washer, I have never used it myself. It can be dangerous to use, especially if you have no idea how to operate it. Besides, you have better things to do than spend your precious time on a $10.00/hr. job, which may end up physically hurting you, or making you sick due to allergic reactions from mold or other contaminants, or damaging your property. Be cautious.

Proven Ways to Increase the Value of Your Property

THE INSIDE

The inside of the house is more critical than the outside. Because this is where your clients are going to spend the majority of their time, it is necessary that the house is neat, clean, and well repaired. You don't want to cut corners when it comes to the bedroom, living room, kitchen, bathrooms, hallways, etc.

PAINT THE HOUSE

Spend some money on painting the house, both on the outside and on the inside. The most important place to start is the outside of the house. Choose exterior paint for the outside, with a flat finish, or whatever finish your maintenance person may recommend for you. This is where your choice of color comes into play. I normally ask questions. I get suggestions from the paint store. Sometimes I visit model homes, of new builds, to see the kind of paint that is being used, mainly on the inside of the home.

My advice to you is to abstain from buying cheap paint. Invest in quality exterior paint. I use Sherwin Williams paint, since independent researchers and industry experts give them high marks and suggest that they make quality products. Quality paint will last longer compared to just choosing any inferior or cheap paint.

Price typically determines the quality of paint to use. So, whether your next exterior-painting project is imminent or a few years off, do not be too shy or too proud to ask for advice. In my case, I also have an interior designer that suggests the colors to use. I am not too proud to say that she is always right on.

When it comes to the inside, make sure that the walls in the family room, the living room, and the bedrooms are all painted. It is always advisable to use neutral and contrasting colors, or appropriate colors. When it comes to the finish of the paint, go with what your heart desires. What I usually like to use is Satin, or Eggshell. Either of these is excellent.

A problem that some investors face is whether to choose water-based or oil-based paint. From my experience, water-based paint is excellent for the exterior of the house. It works well on the siding of the house. It contracts and expands with the siding of the house. It has also been determined that water vapor from inside the house can easily pass through the film of the water-based paint. Oil-based paint, however, is not flexible when it is dry, and can lead to cracks as the siding begins to expand and contract.

GREAT ROOM/LIVING ROOM

Whereas some houses come with a separate family room and a separate living room, some houses come with only a family room. In such a case, we call it a Great Room. Whatever the situation may be, know that this is where families spend most of their time together. Whenever there are visitors and friends, this is where they end up spending the majority of their time: in the great/family room. Careful planning and creativity have to go into repairing the family room.

One of the things that you have to consider is how big you want the family room to be. Can you add more space by knocking down some walls, or are you satisfied with how everything looks currently? If you are satisfied with the space, and all it needs is just painting, then you are good to go. On the other hand, if you cannot see yourself spending more time in the great/family room yourself, due to one reason or another, then you need to come up with some creative ideas to renovate and design it in such a way that it can be very inviting.

Sometimes, if you are fortunate, the family room may come with a fireplace. Please be sure to make the fireplace look neat and clean. If there is no fireplace, discuss with your contractor to see if you can add one. If it can be done without incurring a lot of money, I would advise that you add it. Again, if you cannot see yourself spending more time in the great or family room, then surely, your potential client may not want to spend time there either.

BEDROOM

When it comes to the renovation of bedrooms, make sure that you create a WOW experience. They should be clean, neat, tidy, and peaceful. Secondly, you have to be sure that the bedroom is spacious enough to accommodate furniture that would be placed in there. This, of course, depends on the house and the square footage. Sometimes the bedroom can be so small that the only thing that can fit in there is a small bed and a small dresser. Should this be the case, you may want to check and see if you can knock down some walls to make the room bigger.

If the bedroom is already big and spacious, to your satisfaction, then you need to assess any damages or repairs that need to be taken of. Check the drywall. Are there holes in the wall? How about mold and dew? Do you see any trace of black mold due to moisture? Sometimes there may be some hidden repairs that you may not notice. This is why it is essential to have an expert check to see what needs to be done, and then have them repair the drywall and paint it for you.

The remodeling of bedrooms can sometimes be challenging yet fun. It can also be somewhat basic or expensive. It all boils down to what you want it to be. I will suggest that since this is not going to be your bedroom, do not waste too much money purchasing expensive materials. If you can do the necessary work, yet have it look good, that will be my best advice for you.

The last bedroom that I rehabbed was rather creative. This was a house in a very affluent neighborhood. When I purchased the house, I realized that on the first floor, there was a family room, a living room, a dining room, and another room adjacent to the master bedroom. This room was neither a living room nor a dining room. It was just another room. There was no closet to hang clothes, and nothing was indicating that it could be used for another bedroom. One could use it for a studio or entertainment room, or just a bonus room. I realized, however, that I could convert it into something beneficial that could add value to the house.

Since I didn't know what in the world was going on with that bonus room, I immediately brought in my contractor to give me some ideas as to what we could do differently to add value to the house. He suggested that we convert that room into a bedroom, thereby having two bedrooms on the first floor. This, he said, would give us four bedrooms and two baths. I agreed with his suggestion, and we named it a guest room. Guess what? By converting that bonus room into a very modern bedroom, with all the bells and whistles, which cost me less than a $1,000, I was able to raise the price of the property from $80,000 to $95,000—a profit of $14,000. The best thing was that I had advertised it as a four-bedroom house with two baths, rather than a three-bedroom house with two baths.

Creativity works. If you cannot envision what needs to be done to add more value to your house or property, then bring in a contractor or an interior designer. He or she would give you the best suggestion or recommendation as to what needs to be done. By getting other ideas from a professional, I can seriously tell you that you are bound to reap some good benefits.

BATHROOM

Remodeling a bathroom should never be overlooked when you are fixing the property to sell. Besides the kitchen, which we will discuss shortly, the bathroom renovation should be considered as an investment that will yield almost 100 percent of the cost incurred during resale. It is one of the most crucial selling areas in your property when you plan to put your home on the market. The bathroom should shine. It should be clean. It should be welcoming.

So, the question then is, exactly what should you renovate or improve upon when you redo your bathroom? Before we get into discussing the bathroom, I must tell you that renovating the bathroom is one of the areas where you must spend your renovation money. Just like the family room, people spend a lot of time in the bathroom. You don't want your potential clients to enter your bathroom and come out with huge frowns on their faces, because the bathroom smells like urine and appears so disgusting that no one want to be in there.

You have to do your own assessment to find out what the bathroom looks like. Does it look like a 1960, 1970, or 1980 bathroom? Is it outmoded, archaic, or prehistoric? Does it appear moldy, and you find it difficult to breathe? If this is the case, it must be upgraded. Your bathroom should look modern, fresh, and if at all possible, it should be energy efficient. What this means is that you should consider adding some energy efficient fixtures that will, in the long run, save a lot of money in utilities.

Let us look at the items or fixtures that a bathroom consists of:

Showers, Tubs, and Sinks
If the shower, tub, and sink are not up to par, you may want to get rid of them and install new ones. Not too long ago, in one of my newly purchased properties, I decided to completely remove the sink, tub, and shower, and replace them with something more attractive. I decided to use the most modern style sink for the vanity. The vanity was granite, and it looked fabulously beautiful. Because the bathroom was small and seemed very congested, I got rid of the bathtub and replaced it with a gorgeous, modern-style shower. As easy as it may sound, the decision to completely install new features cost me quite a bit of money. But in the long run, it paid handsomely.

Toilets, Flooring, Lighting
There are so many choices these days when it comes to toilets. The price of toilets can range from $65.00 to $700.00, based on the make and model. As nice as it may seem, I would not suggest that you purchase a $700 toilet for any of your properties, unless it is a high-end luxury home. The highest amount that I spend on my toilets is between $250.00 to $350.00, based on the property and location. In looking for a toilet to purchase, you should consider the following features: efficiency, water usage, flush capacity, seat height, and the shape of the bowl.

As discussed above, your bathroom should be immaculate, pristine, impeccable, neat, and clean. You cannot achieve this goal if the floor is all torn up with holes and appears very old. The choice is up to you. Do you want ceramic or vinyl tiles, wood or stone? How elaborate do you want your floor to look? When it comes to flooring, the sky is the limit. I caution that you guard against overspending.

Be sure that your choice of flooring complements your wall finish. It should be able to handle water and humidity, and it must be slip resistant. Based on my experience, I find that rubber and vinyl can stand up to water very well. Rubber is warm, tough wearing, soft underfoot, easy to maintain, and can be found in any color. However, it can be slippery when wet. If you decide to go with rubber, be sure that your choice can withstand slippery. You can find rubber in either tiles or as one single sheet.

A lot of people use porcelain tiles these days. That is what I have resorted to using in my high-end properties, especially since they are more affordable now than before. Although porcelain tiles may look like ceramic, they are not the same material. I use porcelain tiles because they are resistant to stains, easy to clean, hardwearing, lightweight, and easy to lay (per my contractor), to mention a few, and they add beauty to my bathrooms.

Although a lot of thought does not go into bathroom lighting, I will ask you to seriously consider it as one of the essential items that you want to improve. After all, that is where we start and end our day. It is a place where we relax and have our steam showers. If the lighting is not great, all your efforts in remodeling the bathroom will prove futile.

KITCHEN

If anything will make or break a sale, it is the kitchen. The kitchen is one room that you need to pay a lot of attention to. That is where either the husband or wife spends a lot of time. Moreover, it is the place where the meals are prepared for the family, loved ones, and visitors. The kitchen must be tidy, clean, attractive, modern, up to date, and if possible, without any flaws. An updated kitchen will bring several buyers who would find it difficult to leave the house without presenting you with an offer, assuming the potential buyers are interested in your house.

The features that you replace or install in your kitchen should earn you a tremendous amount of positive return on your investment. To achieve this goal, I will suggest that you choose modern appliances, such as stainless-steel appliances, of high quality. At the time of writing this book, the ongoing demand for potential homeowners is stainless steel appliances. Sears Outlet or Appliance Smart have high-quality, stainless-steel appliances, which are reasonable in price, that you could look into for your properties. But whatever you decide to do, please do not choose cheap or used appliances that may look good but do not function properly. Bear in mind that if you do not use the right appliance for the house you are remodeling, you may not be able to reap the benefits that you desire from it once the house sells. Spend the money and make your kitchen look outstanding.

When it comes to the cabinets in the kitchen, I will suggest that you invest some money to make sure that they look good. The question is, how do you feel about the cabinets when you see them? Are they outdated? If so, can you freshen them up by using Old English, or by painting them to match the décor of the house? Is it worth the risk to salvage them, or will it make investment sense to replace them? These are some questions that you may want your interior designer or contractor to answer for you. If they are too dated to be salvaged, do not hesitate to uninstall and replace them with new ones.

Remember, you want to create a WOW experience for your potential buyers. Once you decide to replace them, be sure to change the knobs and any hardware that is associated with cabinets as well. This will give your kitchen an updated look.

The next thing that you need to look at is your countertop. Great and beautiful countertops can add serious value to your kitchen. If you can afford it, I would suggest for you to choose granite. Several companies, these days, offer some discounts that can help your bottom line. If your search proves futile, be sure to ask your contractor, or a realtor, or search online for companies that are offering discounts on countertops. But if you cannot spend the money because it is too expensive, I will suggest you look for countertops that have patterns that appear like granite.

How about the pantry? Is there one in the house? If there is none, and you have some room where you can create one, consider knocking down some walls to do this. Be sure to install shelves. I am sure that your buyer will be very appreciative.

BASEMENT

The last item that I want to discuss, which many investors overlook, is a finished basement. Believe it or not, finished basements do not only add value to your home and thereby boost your resale value; they add space as well.

Contrary to popular belief, basements are not just for children's playgrounds, or a place to do laundry, or for a workshop. Preferably, it is a place where homeowners can do a myriad of things, especially when it is finished. A finished basement pays very well. These days, whenever someone calls or stops by to view one of my houses, about 80% would always ask for a finished basement. I cannot begin to tell you how many clients I have lost whenever they realize that there is no basement. If a basement is not finished, I would urge you to have a professional work on it, till completion. The conversion could be a deal-breaker.

A lot of people do not pay close attention to what is going on in their basement before finishing it. Some of the things that you should seriously consider are foundation cracks, signs of water or moisture, the absence of a sump pump, backup generator, the plumbing, etc. Be careful to have whatever issues there may be, resolved, before it turns into catastrophic problems, where you end up spending an astronomical amount of money to have all the drywall removed and replaced, just because you failed to do your due diligence, and the basement got flooded.

Although it is essential to finish your basement, do not go investing all your money in it. Statistics has it that it is not worth spending more than 10% of the value of your home when finishing or refinishing your basement. Be sure that whatever amount you invest in your basement would be easily recovered at resale. About 5% to 9% is acceptable, just to be on the safe side of the fence.

The best advice that I received from my mentor, upon discussing how I could reap more benefits from one of my houses, was for me to convert the basement into an apartment. He suggested that I could make it into a comfortable living place for guests, aging parents, or even rent it out to Airbnb clients. Doing this would require that I install a full bathroom (i.e. toilet, sink, shower or bathtub), a full kitchen, a living room, bedroom(s) with closet space, and if possible, a private access, so that in case I rent it out, my tenants would not have to enter and exit the basement through the house itself.

As I mentioned above, before you embark on your basement project, have the foundation walls inspected for moisture. It is also necessary to have your basement insulated. I will suggest that you have a dehumidifier as well. I don't care how savvy your knowledge is regarding construction. When it comes to basements, you may need to hire a professional who will ensure that the right permits are procured, and everything meets code. This will save you money in the long run.

Now that you know how to add value to your property, go quickly to Chapter 8, where we will discuss the best ways to market your properties.

Chapter 8

Proven Ways to Raise Money to Fund Deals

"Money is not the only answer, but it makes a difference"
–Barack Obama

Now that you understand what it means to create wealth, and how you can actually find properties, analyze them, renovate them, and add value to them in order to sell them for a high rate of return, or manage them, the question that you need to ask next is: "How do I fund these deals once I secure them? Or better yet, where do I get the money once I make up my mind to purchase a property?"

Although there are myriads of ways that you can use to fund your deals, I would like for us to look at the following proven ways that I have used in the past, and continue to use, to fund my deals. We will also look at the sources that some of my successful colleagues have used to fund their deals and create massive wealth for themselves.

FINANCIAL INSTITUTIONS

In the broad sense of the word, financial institutions are establishments that focus on, or engage in, transactions such as investments, loans, and deposits.

Financial institutions are comprised of organizations such as banks, insurance companies, investment dealers, and trust companies, just to name a few. Their work covers a broad spectrum that includes receiving deposits of money and giving out loans to clients.

Now that you understand what financial institutions are, and how they function, I would like for us to consider one financial institution in particular, which is commonly used by several people, including myself. This institution is called *the bank*.

Banks

According to the dictionary, a bank is defined as *an establishment that is authorized by a government to accept deposits, pay interest, clear checks, make loans, and act as an intermediary in financial situations.*

Since the subprime lending that collapsed in 2007/2008, lending requirements have become very cumbersome and stringent. Real estate investors, as well as some homeowners, have found it very difficult to obtain loans and/or mortgages from banks. Before 2007, all you had to do was fog up a mirror, and you were granted a loan or a mortgage to fund your deals. This is no longer the case. The bar has been raised very high.

These days, you have to have an excellent credit score, be the W-2 wage earner, your income to debt ratio has to be perfect, and the list goes on and on. Sometimes, even after you have spent sleepless nights gathering and supplying all the documents that the financial institution has requested from you, you may be shocked to realize that you have been denied after all.

If you are not careful, this could become a devastating blow to you, and shatter your spirit, your aspirations, and goals, to pieces. This is where I want to sound the warning bell, to encourage you to stay in the game and not to allow one thing to take you off course. Do not pack your bags and leave. Some of these things just come to shake you, but you must stay the course. Whenever things like this happen, remember that it only comes to test your faith, your strength, and your ability to overcome obstacles.

If, on the other hand, you are fortunate enough to be approved, do not forget your experience. Remember all the hoops that you had to go through to obtain that loan.

Due to all the difficulties, processes, and the length of time that is involved in dealing with the banks, it is essential for you to look at other creative ways to get money to fund your deals. The chances are that if you only depend on the banks, a time may come where you would be very disappointed, and you may end up losing a deal that you sweated to secure.

With that said, let's look at other various ways that you can fund your deals so that you can start to create wealth.

HARD MONEY LOANS

Hard money loans are asset-based financing that you can get from certain individuals. Such individuals have lots of money. Other hard money lenders could be financial institutions as well. As the name suggests, hard money lenders are very strict, and they tend to have rigid and sometimes inflexible requirements. Before you are approved for hard money, the lender would typically look at your deal and analyze it to the letter. Sometimes they would come to the property or the house that you need the money for. He or she would walk through the property and scrutinize it, evaluate it, and examine it, and then decide if they are going to fund your deal.

My first property was funded with hard money. Although I received the money that I wanted, and was able to close the deal, I was extremely frustrated with the process. The lender came to the property, walked through it and analyzed it, and issued some threats, with the assurance that if I did not make the interest payments and the principal amount at the time agreed, they would end up taking the property from me, ruin my credit, and NEVER lend to me again. Since it was my first deal, and I did not want to lose it, I went ahead and signed on the dotted line. Even though the interest rate was very high, and it was an interest-only loan, I still ended up with an outstanding profit. As hard as these lenders can be, do not let that stop you from borrowing from them if there is no other way to fund your deal.

Interest Rates for Hard Money

As explained above, when it comes to hard money, interest rates are higher than conventional loans. You have to understand that most hard money loans are used for a short period of time, sometimes just for three months, or between 6 to 12 months. You have to negotiate the terms of the loan with the lender. It is similar to what is known as a *bridge loan*, which serves as interim financing for an individual or business, until they obtain permanent financing. From my example above, you can see that the interest rate granted to me was very high. Not only that, there are points that are assessed and, on most occasions, other costs and fees are added as well. Don't be surprised if you encounter miscellaneous fees before the loan gets in your hands.

Qualifications/Requirements for Hard Money Loan

The qualifying criteria for a hard money loan are different from lender to lender. Primarily, it depends on the lender. There are hard money lenders who may lend to you based on the after-repair value of the property. Some would qualify you based on what you specifically need the money for (e.g., purchase and repair).

Some may or may not lend to you if they realize that you need the money to refinance a property that you already own. Others may or may not lend

to you if you need the money to purchase a primary residence. Most will lend to you if they know that you need the money to purchase a property, rehab it, and then sell it within a certain specified time frame. What this should tell you is that the purpose for which you want the loan in the first place plays a vital role.

Other Qualifying Criteria

Although not everyone requires a credit score, some of the lenders look at credit scores very closely. Before the 2007/2008 subprime loan debacle, one could have a credit score of 500 and would still be granted a handsome amount of money to do deals. All you needed was what was known as stated income, without any verification. They also looked at other conventional lending criteria with their eyes closed (they never took your qualification seriously). In other words, most hard money lenders would qualify you for a loan based on the value of the real estate that is being collateralized. Today, your credit score has to be over and above 620 or 640 for hard money lenders to consider you.

(Low LTV: Loan to Value)

On many occasions, the most significant amount that you could expect would be between 65% and 70% of the after-repair value of the property. For example, if the after-repair value is $200,000, the lender may loan you between $130,000–$140,000. You will then be required to come to closing with the difference as down payment. This is because he or she wants to have added security, just in case you default, and they have to foreclose on the property. So, one has to be very careful as to how they go about using hard money loans. Again, I have used it before. It was not fun.

CREDIT CARDS

One other way to fund your deals is through the use of credit cards. Whereas other means of raising funds can get you far in real estate investing, the use of credit cards may only get you so far. What do I mean by this? Although the use of credit cards can be very instrumental, it is not in all cases that you can depend on credit cards to fund your deals, due to the limitation of the balance that you may have on it.

Assuming you have a credit limit of $20,000, that amount in itself will not be sufficient to close on a house with a higher purchase price. You can, however, use a credit card for down payments on your purchases, or to do repairs, or to pay for closing costs.

With all that said, it is even possible that you may still be able to use your credit card to purchase a house in some cities, where the price of properties is not too high.

So, one has to be very creative in using this type of funding. If your rental unit is only bringing you 10% return on investment (ROI), but the credit company is charging you 20% interest, nothing should push you to enter into such a contract, knowing that you would just be digging a hole for yourself. You will end up having negative cash flows as opposed to positive cash flows. If, on the other hand, the numbers look different, where you are positively cash flowing, then, by all means, go for it.

PARTNERSHIPS

Another way that you could raise funds would be to bring a partner on board. Once you bring a partner, you must decide what kind of partnership you are going to form with this individual(s). Be sure to put everything on paper. If you do not have everything in writing, your partnership may become very ugly, and you and your partner may end up hating the partnership. Once the contract is in place, have an attorney review every detail of it. It will save you in the long run.

What kind of partnership should you have?

It depends. Some partners may want to split the deal with you 50/50. Others may want to be what is known as "silent or passive partners." In other words, they don't want to have anything to do with the day to day running of your company. They would rather sit and have you do everything, and then pay them when the house is sold, according to the terms of the contract.

I must tell you, however, that partnership can sometimes be very expensive as well. Whereas it is a good thing to have somebody who will bring some or all of the money to fund your deals, remember that you are the one that still controls the deal. So, you get to decide what the deal should be. Either 60/40 (i.e. you get 60%, and your partner receives 40% of the profit, or alternatively, it could be 70/30, 50/50, or whatever you want it to be.

Whenever you bring a partner to fund your deals, do not look at yourself as a beggar. Remember, you did all the hard work by locating the property, presenting the offer, having your offer accepted, analyzing the deal, and coming up with estimated repairs— and then offering someone the opportunity to come on board with you as a partner, to share the profit to be harvested from this deal that you put together. In absolute no terms should you look at yourself as inferior to whomever you bring on board.

Due to lack of money, some real estate investors think that they are subordinates to their money partners. My advice to you is that if you present an opportunity to someone to come on board with you because they can fund the deal, but they end up rejecting your offer, please do not be devastated, discouraged, or disappointed. If he is not interested, show them the door.

There are plenty of people waiting to be presented with opportunities that would help them to make more money than the banks are offering for their savings, certificate of deposits, the stock market, etc.

Adopt the motto, S W S W S W S W: "Some Will; Some Won't; So What? Someone's Waiting." Memorize this model; ingrain it in your head, and do not allow anybody to get you down to the point where you are giving up on your path to success in creating the wealth of your dreams.

After all, how much are the banks paying today in interest rates? It is negligible. They should be thankful to you for opening the door to them to make money. They need to treat you with respect, just like you will also treat them with the respect that is due them.

So, what do I do since the sources of funds discussed above are expensive and pricey? I am glad you asked. Let us explore further and look at another source of funding our deals. This is my favorite:

PRIVATE FUNDS

Reasons you need private funds for your real estate investment:

1. When you have private funds, you can make cash offers with confidence.

2. When you have private funds, you can be very flexible with terms.
3. When you have private funds, you will not incur the expensive rates that partners may want from you. In this case, private funds are cheaper than having a partner(s).
4. When you have private funds, you don't have to use your credit, and will not have to put your name on any loan document belonging to a financial institution.
5. When you have private funds, your worries about cash flow problems would be eliminated.
6. When you have private funds, you can make offers on deals, and close on them quickly. Private funds help you to build excellent relationships with real estate agents. They would trust you and bring you more deals, over and over again, just because they know that you can close on deals without any problem.

So, What Exactly is Private Money (Funds)?

Whenever you borrow money from a friend or a relative, or from an individual instead of from a bank or a financial institution, it is considered private funds. The amount could come from their savings, IRA, or 401K.

Sources of Private Money

The first thing you must think about is, "Who do I know to approach with my ideas so that they can invest in my business?"

Whereas there are so many ways that you can find private lenders, my advice to you is, to begin with, your relatives, friends, or what you would call your inner circle or warm market. Start with them first. These are your parents, siblings, grandparents, neighbors across the street, friends, family physicians, dentists, eye doctors, fellow workers, your lawyer, your accountant, your admin, or other real estate investors from your Real Estate Investment Association (REIA). You would be surprised that these individuals have money that you do not know of.

Recently, I discussed with a friend of mine, who is also a real estate investor. He was casually talking to his uncle, when out of the blue, his uncle Jack asked him: "So, what do you do?" "I invest in real estate by using private money from some of my coworkers, as well as some friends." Then, Uncle Jack continued with his interrogation. "Have you considered asking any of your relatives?"

"Not really," I answered, "Because I do not want them to judge me and discourage me from my pursuit of happiness."

"How much return on investment do you currently pay?" asked Uncle Jack. In the final analysis, Uncle Jack invested $200,000 in his nephew's business. My friend was so happy that he started asking for money from his family members. That one investment from his uncle propelled his company, and gave him the confidence to do well and invest in more properties.

Proven Ways to Raise Money to Fund Deals

I know this can be a complicated process for some, since we don't want our parents, friends, or other relatives to think that we depend on them for money for our businesses. Because of this justified or unjustified fear, you must think about how to approach a relative.

Before you approach a family member, you'll need to change your way of thinking, by not thinking that you are just going to beg for money. Instead, they must realize that you are presenting them with a business opportunity that would help them. You must come from the position of opportunity provider.

Also, let it be settled in your mind that you are instead extending an invitation to a relative to make them money. Indeed, you are going to help them to make more money than they are currently building on their investments (e.g., certificates of deposits in the bank, savings account, IRAs that are not yielding any substantial returns). They, on the other hand, must count themselves fortunate that you are presenting them with a business offer that would enable them to make more money.

Nowadays, the banks are only paying anywhere from half to 1.5 percent interest rate on loans. So, when you approach a relative, let them realize that you are willing to pay them over and above what they are currently earning from their financial institutions. If someone is receiving 1.5%, try to double it, or even raise the bar and pay him or her about 6% to 8%.

You must be creative when it comes to raising capital to fund your deals. If you want to depend on financial institutions to fund your deals, I can assure you that there may come a time when the banks will not look at you positively any longer. They have limitations as to how much they can give to you at a given time. Sometimes the process could be arduous and tasking.

As discussed earlier, sometimes you may provide several documents to the banks, just to find out that you have not been approved for the loan that you requested. If you are not strong enough, these kinds of disappointments may discourage you. It can break your spirit and end your dream of becoming a real estate entrepreneur. It, therefore, behooves you to look at all the sources of funds mentioned above, and decide which one works for you. It is critical. It is crucial. It is essential for your business. This is the lifeblood that will give life to your business and propel you to create wealth.

The question that may be looming in your mind now is, "Where and how do I find private money, since I do not have wealthy relatives or wealthy friends?" I heard you loud and clear, and I am glad you asked. I have some great suggestions for you. Let us discuss them:

DIRECT MAILING

One way to find private lenders is through a list broker. This is where you obtain a list of investors with money. Some of these individuals have cash sitting in banks but hardly yielding any returns for them. By sending out direct mail to certificate of deposit (CD) holders, people with retirement accounts, IRA or 401K, and to the retired who are currently on fixed income, as well as the self-employed, or people with money market accounts, just to mention a few, you are assured to possibly get someone that can buy into your vision and provide you with the money that you need.

Secondly, you can advertise in the newspapers. You must, however, check with the Security Exchange Commission (SEC) to be sure you are operating within the law. This is a very serious process, so please do not ignore it. There are specific SEC laws, regulations, and guidance regarding advertising for private funds. One of the requirements is that you must be registered with the SEC before you can advertise.

Thirdly, one of the best strategies that I have used in the past, and continue to use today, in getting my potential lenders hooked up, is through luncheons. I hear you loud and clear: "Who is going to pay for that?"

My answer: "YOU." Yes, you have to invite them to a free luncheon, where you can provide them with the necessary information about your plans, goals, and aspirations. Give them examples of what you have done in the past, what you are doing currently, and what you are planning to do in the future. You must answer the question as to why they should invest with you. They must feel secure that they are not going to lose their money once they invest with you. To prove that, you must be willing to explain to them that you would give them the following items once they decide to jump on board with you:

1. A promissory note
2. A deed
3. A mortgage
4. Insurance or title insurance
5. Appraisal of the property
6. Inspection report
7. UCC-1 filing (UCC-1 stands for Uniform Commercial Code-1. It is a legal form that a creditor will file to give public notice that he or she has an interest in the property of a person who owes a debt to the creditor, as emphatically stated in the agreement or contract that is creating the debt. This filing alerts the public to know of the secured investment).

The onus is on you to let them know what and how you are going to pay their interest rate, the minimum investment you are willing to accept, and how long you plan to hold their money, whether it is for a year, two years, or after the property sells. Are you going to pay interest rates monthly, quarterly, semi-annually, or annually, etc.? All these should be questions that you already have answers to, before hosting the luncheon.

Above all, and in all your dealings, remember that you must show yourself as being credible, whether it is at a luncheon or a one-on-one presentation. It is a necessary fact that you should have a Credibility Kit, with information about you and your company, and how you started to invest in real estate.

Have you done deals in the past? Tell them about how you purchased the properties, how you funded them, and how you paid back the principle and the interest rate. I recommend that you have the before and after repairs pictures of some of your properties, available for them to see. This would alleviate their fears.

GO GET THEM!

Chapter 9

Best Ways to Market and Sell Your Properties (Part 1)

> *"The aim of marketing is to know and understand the customer so well the product or service fits him and sells itself."*
> – Peter Drucker

Although marketing and selling your house can be taxing, there are several proven ways that you can accomplish your goal for huge profits. Let us explore the best ways that you can market your house with or without your involvement. We will look at what works best in this market, and the resources that are readily available to you, which if employed, can increase your ROI (return on investment) tremendously.

REAL ESTATE AGENT

One of the proven ways to market and sell your house is to use a real estate agent. Realtor(s) or real estate agents have access to the MLS, and on many occasions, have an idea of who may be in the market looking for properties to sell and/or buy. The MLS, as we have discussed before, gives the best exposure to your market. Anyone with access to this system can see all the available listed properties in your market. It, therefore, behooves you to have your property listed in the MLS, so that you can quickly market and sell it as fast as possible.

A word of caution:

Before you go out searching for a realtor, you need to know that all real estate agents are not created equal. Whereas some are willing, and will go beyond the call of duty, others will eagerly list your property, and then leave it there to market and sell itself. To avoid this from happening to you, there are some qualities and qualifications that I want you to look for in an agent, before you end up giving your property to him or her to market and sell on your behalf.

Look for an agent that is *professional*

To market and sell your property, do not just look for someone who claims to be a real estate agent. A professional agent would not look any way they desire to look when showing your property. Realtors who show up wearing shabby clothes, and are not well groomed, should be a negative flag for you.

A professional realtor must look very attractive to be taken seriously. When I meet with clients, I don't care if the property I am showing is a high end or a low end. I look my best. I do not just slap on jeans and sneakers to meet my potential clients. To me, that is a deal killer. I must be taken seriously. If I want to be taken seriously, then definitely, my hired realtor should also be taken seriously.

Look for an agent that is *punctual*

There are those who do not have the respect of their time, and for that matter do not respect another person's time either. The question that you may want to ask and answer genuinely is: "How punctual do I want the agent to be when marketing and selling my property?" It is the most frustrating and exasperating trait to have. It is a big No in my books for an agent to be 5 minutes late to meet and show my property to a potential client. If I can get very annoyed when a buyer strolls in 5 minutes late, how much more annoying is it when the agent is always late when showing my property?

Before I meet a client, I call to make sure that they have the address to the property, and that they can easily find the house slated for sale. If not, I help them out, even if I have to give them directions step by step. This is because my time is my most valuable asset, and I do not play with it.

In this technological world of today, most people have cell phones with navigation systems that come with the phones, such as Google Maps, Wave, etc. If a client shows up ten minutes late, I do not take them seriously because, in my mind, they are just there for other reasons, and not to consider my property seriously.

Based on the reasons mentioned above, I expect my real estate agent to have the utmost respect for others, and to show up on the property at least 15 to 20 minutes before a potential buyer shows up. If I cannot get that commitment from an agent, I look for another agent, who is hungry and would be punctual no matter the circumstances.

Look for an agent that has *experience*

Any realtor can tell you that they have the experience to market and sell your house. My question always is: "Do you have proven results to show me that you actually and sincerely possess the experience and capacity needed to execute the task at hand?" If the answer is yes, I request proof of past sales. How many houses did they list during the course of last year, and how many homes were they successful in selling? How long did the house stay on the market? All these are excellent questions that will give you an idea as to whom you are dealing with.

Besides their job as a real estate agent, do they have another job that takes them away from time to time, and thereby are not focusing on your property? What is their success rate regarding houses that they were able to list? Was it 20%, 50%, or 90%? It is up to you, the investor, to define success rate. In my case, if you are not within the 80% to 100% range, I look for someone with a proven, higher success rate.

I don't have the time for any of my properties to be used for experimental purposes. Remember, time is money, and the more successful transactions a real estate agent can handle, the better they will market and sell your property at lightning speed.

Look for an agent that can *communicate*

In my haste to sell one of my properties, as a newbie (new investor), I agreed to have this real estate agent, whose name I will not disclose, market and sell my house for me. Although he was not my first choice, I yielded to his consistent and forceful, needy plea. He was close to tears when I initially told him that I could not hand over my property to him. He went on by explaining how he would lose his license if he did not market and sell my house. On top of all of that begging, he vowed to sell it within ninety days at the most. He was incredibly emotional, and he sincerely got my sympathy. Needless to say, as soon as I signed the contract, and he placed his big sign in my yard, I did not hear from him until after a month had elapsed. To tell you the truth, I called the Board of Realtors to inquire as to whether that guy was indeed a real estate agent.

Frequent and constant communication should be one of your requirements when looking for an agent. I demand consistent updates and feedback from my agents. If an agent lacks in this department, I immediately bring our relationship to a halt. If the agent does not communicate with you, how much more would he communicate with a buyer who may be interested in your house, and would need a push from him to help them make up their mind in choosing your house?

Look for an agent with *excellent negotiation skills*

As you may already know, realtors make their money from commissions after they sell a property. The size of the commission check depends on how much they can sell a house for. Since this is true, an outstanding realtor will then do whatever he or she can to get as much money as possible for you, the investor. A good realtor will not only be interested in the commission that they make, but will also be concerned about the money that they end up bringing to you, the property owner.

This characteristic does not come easily. Sadly to say, it is not every real estate agent that possesses it. The onus is on you, the investor, to comb through as many realtors as you can, to find the one with excellent negotiation skills; one who will go beyond the call of duty and make sure that you are satisfied with your profit before they agree to sell the house at a particular price. The agent will always communicate with you before they send in a counter offer, to be sure that you are satisfied and happy.

Look for an agent that is *very creative*

One area that you must consider critical is that of creativity. If the agent that you hire has no trace of creativity, then I can assure you that you are seriously dealing with the wrong person.

Best Ways to Market and Sell Your Properties (Part 1)

As explained above, during my early years in real estate investing, I gave my house to a realtor who just placed a sign in the front yard. As far as I know, that was all the marketing that he did. He did not just waste my time but also robbed me of a buyer that could have purchased my home at a handsome price, had he sincerely marketed my property creatively.

Marketing a house is crucial and should be taken very seriously. How he or she describes your house, the kind of pictures that are taken and used as a marketing tool, the sort of advertisements, the strategies that are put in place, etc., are all very important when it comes to marketing and selling your house.

If your agent does not possess these critical qualities, my friend, you are just barking up the wrong tree. Look through the forest and choose the tree that would be on fire for you—not just someone who takes horrible pictures and won't use a professional photographer to take the pictures, even if they lack in that area. No matter what you do, the skill of creativity is one of the serious yardsticks that you will use in hiring an agent to market and sell a house for you.

Honesty and Good Reputation

The wisest man that ever lived, King Solomon, gave us a very good admonishment in the bible. You can find the text in Proverbs 22:1: *"Choose a good reputation over great riches; being held in high esteem is better than silver or gold."* Having a good name is extremely important. We have some realtors that lack gravely when it comes to honesty and good reputation.

Although I will typically ask about a particular realtor, it is not always easy to tell when a person is being honest or stretching the truth. One of the ways that I find out as to whether someone is telling the truth or being dishonest is to request new sales contacts and/or recent testimonials from clients. If they give me the go-ahead to contact some of their previous clients, I do that to be sure that I am dealing with an honest person.

If the realtor has been an excellent agent with a good reputation, the people that I contact for reference would tell me what they know about the agent. However, if on the other hand, they refuse to inform me of their relationship with the agent, or if they have no comments, I take that answer to mean, "Please be cautious."

The worse thing to happen is for the agent to refuse to give you references. If the realtor refuses to honor my request, and has no testimonials, I do not hire him or her. I continue to search until I find one with a good name and a good reputation.

FOR SALE BY OWNER (FSBO)

If I have not yet convinced you to hire a real estate agent to work diligently to market and sell your property, but you would instead undertake the responsibility upon yourself and accomplish the task at hand, then I have the following suggestions for you to consider, in generating the highest return on investment.

One way that you can market and sell your property is known as FSBO (For Sale by Owner).

For Sale by Owner is when a seller decides to do his or her marketing, and then sell the house without the help of a realtor. Since there is no agent involved, the seller may find it difficult to list the property in the MLS, unless the seller is granted access through other means.

Although there are several ways that you could list your property in the MLS, it is not easy, and it could end up costing you quite a bit of money to have it done for you. However, if you insist on listing it in the MLS, I would suggest that you try the following proven ways:

How to List Your House in the MLS as a FSBO

Before you do a flat fee listing, be sure to price your property competitively. If you have a friend who happens to be a realtor, you can ask him to give you an idea of what your house could sell for, by doing a competitive market analysis for you. This would give you an idea as to how to price your house.

You can also use the Internet to obtain an idea of what your house should sell for. There are several sites on the Internet that you can use in this regard. One of the sites is called Zillow. The reason I am asking you to price your house competitively is to help you from overpricing or underpricing your house. Overpricing your home may have your house stay on the market for a long time without selling.

Once you are comfortable with the price, look for a way to have your house listed in the MLS through flat fee listing.

There are several real estate agents who may be willing to place your property in the MLS for a flat fee. This fee is paid up front. The fee would be the only amount that you are required to pay, unless you negotiate for something else with the agent.

Once agreed upon, you do not have to pay the agent commission when the house sells. Your house would be listed in the MLS as soon as the amount quoted by the agent is paid. Unless your property sells faster, it will remain in the MLS for about six months or more.

How to Market Your House as a FSBO

Should you decide to have your property placed in the MLS through a flat fee listing service, I would encourage you to put a FOR SALE BY OWNER sign in front of your house. The sign should have your telephone number, your website address, or any other information that would be helpful to buyers. In this way, you would be contacted quickly by interested parties. Be sure that the sign is visible so that anyone that passes by can see it.

Best Ways to Market and Sell Your Properties (Part 1)

Since you are marketing the house by yourself, be sure to have the information about the house in a brochure, and place it beside the sign in the yard. The advertisement should have information about the number of bedrooms and bathrooms, the square footage of the house, the price of the house, the details of the house, including dining room, living room, fireplace (if any), the type of flooring, etc. This is beneficial to you personally, and will cut down on all the *time wasters* who might call.

You can also use the following websites to market your house:

- Craigslist.com
- ForSaleByOwner.com
- HomesByOwner.com
- Zillow.com
- Owners.com

How to Show Your Property as a FSBO

Once you place your house in the MLS, and have placed a sign in the front yard, and have printed and distributed some brochures, you should be ready to receive and answer calls. Most of the calls that you will receive may likely come from curious individuals, who will request to view your property. What I have done, and continue to do today, is to place a lockbox either on the front door or the back door of the house. Inside the lockbox is a key to the house. The reason why you want to consider this is because you will save yourself the heartache of going to show the property anytime anyone calls to inquire about it.

Secondly, some of the calls may come from real estate agents who may want to *coop* with you. This means that the realtor may request that you pay them a partial commission when they bring you a buyer. With a realtor showing your property, all you will have to do is to grant them access by giving them the code to your lockbox.

Be careful not to give the code to just anyone that identifies themselves as a realtor. Do your due diligence by verifying the identity of the real estate agent before providing the code to your lockbox. Obtaining feedback from the agent, after showing your property, is necessary. This process will keep you updated, and you will know as to whether the potential buyer is interested or not interested in purchasing your house.

FSBO Pros:

A. No agent commission of 6%–7%. If the sales price of your house is $200,000, you will be saving about $12,000 to $14,000, which will go directly into your pocket rather than giving it to a realtor.
B. You are always in control. You decide on the price, the scheduling times, and how you negotiate with a buyer.
C. You get to choose the time allowed for interested buyers to walk through your house.
D. You know your house better than any real estate

professional, so you can highlight all the amenities or the highest selling points of the house to the potential buyer.

E. You can choose the publications to place in your house for marketing purposes. A real estate professional will have to try to remember all the features of your house, along with all the other houses that he or she is currently trying to sell.

FSBO Cons:

A. In some cases, when the potential buyer realizes that you are selling the house without a real estate professional, you may run the risk of selling your house for a lot less than it's worth. Statistics have shown that the average For Sale by Owner home sells for about 15% less than homes sold through a realtor.

B. Your house may not be as visible as you want it, if listed with a real estate professional. The reason is that some realtors may not advertise or promote your house outside the Multiple Listing Service (MLS).

C. You may have to pay an attorney to prepare all the legal forms, disclosures, and other documents needed to have your client sign when the house sells. All these responsibilities fall on you whenever you decide to use this kind of strategy to market and sell your house. Without the proper disclosures and the appropriate documentation, you run the risk of financial and legal liability.

D. You'll have to spend some time educating yourself on the process of selling a house, the current market, advertising methods, and working with potential buyers.

E. Sometimes it can be difficult to weed out unqualified or uninterested buyers. Unfortunately, people who are unable obtain the proper financing will look for houses that are FSBO, because they know most private sellers are inexperienced. You'll also get some *just curious* folks, who are not serious about buying a home but like to look around. These types of inquiries will waste a lot of your time, and can distract you from serious buyers.

F. I would advise you not to be discouraged by all these negative aspects, should you decide to list your home as FSBO. You need to go into the process informed and educated. Do your research, prepare for the pitfalls and roadblocks, and don't spend dollars to save pennies.

How to Perform Your Negotiations as a FSBO

Real estate negotiations take the form of a contract that is submitted to you, the seller. You have the right to either accept, revise, or reject the offer. Your intention should be made known and presented to the buyer within a specified time frame. The process continues until both parties reach an agreement and the contract is signed.

In most states, there is a standard sales and purchase agreement for real estate. You can have your attorney review the contract to be sure all the i's are dotted, and all the t's are crossed. On the other hand, you can find a real estate agent that will perform this function for you, for a negotiated fee.

Having gone through this process before, I was able to consult with family members who were real estate agents and attorneys, and then negotiate with the other party to sell my home.

Agents like to close deals quickly so they can get their commission, even if you don't ultimately receive the price you want for your home. They may inadvertently relay your negotiating position to the buyer. If you are a distressed seller, then that is the last thing you would ever want an enthusiastic buyer to know. Doing your own negotiating ensures that you do not give away essential indications of your financial strengths and weaknesses.

How to Comply with Real Estate Laws in Your Area

It's critical that you comply with the laws in your state. Some of the laws are universal and will apply to the sale of your house, no matter where you live. The Fair Housing Act stipulates that sellers not be allowed to discriminate against buyers for reasons including race, religion, and sex.

Although there are several templates for contracts and agreements, which you can find online that may help you to get started with the selling process, you need to know that such forms are not always specific to your unique situation. It is best to have a real estate attorney review all the documents and contracts related to the sale of your home, before signing on the dotted line.

FINAL WORD

One thing that you should know is that selling a house is not for everyone. This is because many individuals may not have the time or the patience to deal with the whole process of selling a house. For some, if the listing price is low enough, the potential profit to be realized may not be worth the time they may be willing to invest in selling the house without a realtor.

Whatever the case may be, consider the enormous profits that you could enjoy by selling the house on your own. If you know something about real estate, and can do some of the work on your own, you may end up saving a tremendous amount of money, resulting in more profit, by selling your personal property.

Chapter 10

Best Ways to Market and Sell Your Properties (Part 2)

PHOTOGRAPHS

Photograph the Front

Pictures speak volumes. It is therefore important and crucial that you take this very seriously. In this age of technology, most home buyers do not read the newspapers, let alone look for houses listed for sale in the newspapers. I will argue that those that read the newspapers are in the minority. People who are seriously shopping for their next dream home will definitely shop online or go through a real estate agent with access to the MLS. As you may agree, the use of the Internet has become so prevalent that many people would use it for anything, including searching for their next home.

For you to make a positive impact, you need to have great pictures of the property that you want to list and sell. Without good pictures, you may not have the positive results that you are looking for. Great and perfect photos are essential to marketing and selling anything, including houses. Listings that have no pictures are most of the time passed over and ignored. I don't care how long it takes. People who are seriously looking for their next home would take their time to comb through quite a number of photos on the Internet, before selecting the right house(s), which they would want to see before entering into a contract. Do not take this advice for granted. You need to be aware of what your competition is doing, and do better to exceed them.

Here are some suggestions to consider when taking photos of your house to market and sell.

- The pictures should not show sidewalks and streets. Crop them out.
- Make sure that you park your car on the road when taking photos of the house. Try not to park in the driveway or in front of the house.
- Whereas I am not asking you to go and purchase a costly camera, you need to obtain a decent one that can shoot up close and angled pictures.
- If you are not great at taking pictures, my suggestion for you is to hire a professional photographer to assist you in this department. I can tell you that using a professional photographer can quickly generate many leads for you in a short time.
- Before you take pictures of your house, be sure to trim or cut any tall bushes that may hinder your progress. Completely eradicate branches from a tree that may block your front door.

Best Ways to Market and Sell Your Properties (Part 2)

Other Exterior Photographs

As you take pictures of the front of the house, do not ignore the sides and the back of the house. Also, be sure to take photos of the yard, private fence, pool in the back if any, playground, etc. Why is this important? It's because your potential clients would love to see every picture of your property. The more pictures they see, the better the speed of their decision to view your house and present you with an offer.

Be sure to:

- Emphasize the amount of space 0r the square footage of your property.
- Mow the lawn and trim the bushes neatly.
- Remove evidence of pets.
- Put away all children's toys.
- Avoid shooting in the sun.

Interior Photographs

It would serve you well to take pictures of every room. Do not allow the lack of light in the interior rooms to deter you from taking pictures. Once taken, you can enhance the pictures, and they would look fantastic and to your liking.

Before you take the interior room pictures, be sure to:

- Open all the drapes and/or blinds.

- Turn on all the lights to illuminate the rooms.
- Have the floors cleaned professionally, and then focus on all the intricate details. (An example of this would be the condition of the wood flooring, and/or other exciting things, like the fireplace, etc.)
- Do not have any trash cans, bottles, etc. showing up in the pictures.
- Close all toilets in the bathrooms.
- Staging the house goes a very long way. Consider floral arrangements in kitchens, dining rooms, and family rooms.
- Avoid shooting into mirrors because your image will reflect.

VIRTUAL TOURS

Virtual tours of a house is one of the best ways to showcase your property. It would get your potential buyers excited. With the help of a video camera, you can go from room to room to videotape the décor of the bedrooms, master suite, family room, living room, dining room, and kitchen, after the house is staged.

Secondly, should the house be vacant, be sure to carry out the same exercise as mentioned above, from room to room. In this regard, your focus should be on the size of the bedrooms, master suite, family room, living room, dining room, and kitchen. Virtual tours intrigue buyers and help them to make faster decisions. Be sure not to deny your clients the excitement.

Thirdly, it is good to know that virtual tours will grab a buyer by the hand and lead him or her from room to room. You can hire a tour company to do this for you if you are not able to do it yourself. To make it lively, it would be great to add some soft or soothing music, and a written description of whatever you are showing or videotaping at the time of the tour.

CLASSIFIED ADS

Although many people have turned to the Internet for research and other reasons, quite a few people still believe that the newspapers have relevant and current information, no matter what. In my neighborhood, newspapers are delivered to my neighbors every single day. There are people who, because of their busy lifestyle, will instead get all that they need in the Sunday newspapers. This is where they spend much time going through the classifieds to pick and choose what they need. I am saying this so that your focus will not only be limited to the Internet but in other areas of advertisement as well.

Following are the steps that you need to take before you place an advertisement(s) in the classified ads section of a newspaper:

1. You need to call the newspaper company in your city to find out what they would charge you.
2. It is essential to know that the company will charge you based on specific variables.
3. You need to know the number of lines that will be going into your advertisement. Is it three lines, four, or five lines?
4. You need to know the number of words that will be going into your ad.

5. You need to know the number of pictures that you will place in the newspapers.
6. You need to know that there will be a charge for the setting, the font, the style, etc.
7. The more lines that you place in the newspapers in the classified section, the more money you will have to pay.
8. You need to know that if you use the same newspapers repeatedly, the chances are that the company may give you a terrific discount, especially if you decide to open an account for your company.

I have used the classified ads section of the newspapers on different occasions to search for properties that I wanted to purchase. I have also used it to sell properties. To date, I have not regretted using the newspapers. It has worked very well for me. I, therefore, do not advise you against using the classifieds, because it will be worth your while.

It's always good to ask questions, or get suggestions from the sales agent of the newspaper company, to see where to place your advertisement. The section in which you put your ad may also depend on what you are interested in doing. Do you want a straight rent, or are you going to lease with an option purchase? For example, if you are selling the house, then you may want to place the advertisement in the For Sale by Owner section. If you are renting the house, then you may want to put it under the Rent section of the classifieds. I have seen it in both ways, where investors would typically list the house, no matter what, either in the For Sale or For Rent section.

Best Ways to Market and Sell Your Properties (Part 2)

FLYERS

Flyers are another means that you can use to market your house. The reason why my company has used flyers in the past, and continue to use them, is that they work well! Flyers have proven to be a beneficial way to get your message across.

Secondly, they are very cost-effective in advertising, and can generate a high return on investment for you. In case you cannot print your flyers, I would advise you to look for a professional printer or company. Some companies specialize in designing and printing flyers, at a cheaper rate that you would appreciate.

Thirdly, flyers are very easy to handle and distribute. I will never forget going to a house and finding one of my flyers on their refrigerator. Because flyers tend to be very small, they can quickly be passed on to friends or family members. Your relatives may find it easy to pass your flyers on to other family members who may be in need of houses.

Besides, I find it easy to distribute them. You can quickly place them in strategic areas, like laundry mats, stores, gyms, restaurants, cafes, schools, and other vital areas.

Spend some time thinking about where your potential clients spend their time, then get moving! You'll be surprised at how many cafés, stores, gyms, restaurants, schools, and other businesses are happy to help you connect with potential clients. Ask favorite local spots to post some of your flyers on notice boards or in diverse areas, and they will gladly do that for you. Just sit back and wait for the magic to happen.

Stand Out with Your Flyers

Be sure that your flyers are not cheap looking. They should stand out from your competition. How do you do that? *By not having your flyers look like junk mail.* Always use the highest quality paper that you can find on the market. A company like VistaPrint.com can give you some very professional and quality flyers. Fedex/Kinkos, Office Depot, Staples, and other printing companies can provide you with very high professional quality flyers. If possible, avoid the temptation to DIY (do it yourself).

As you develop or design your flyers to distribute, do not forget to have a lovely picture of your house embedded in it. Also, highlight the important things or beautiful items in your home to compel your potential buyer emotionally. Please try as much as possible to avoid the temptation of not having good pictures of your house on the flyer. As I indicated above, the front of the house should be well kept and trimmed nicely. Make sure there is no peeling paint or broken branches or trees. It is imperative that all of that be fixed professionally so that the picture on your flyer would instead tell the story, as opposed to you telling the story about your house.

Best Ways to Market and Sell Your Properties (Part 2)

POST CARDS

People ask me all the time as to the size of a postcard to use—whether they should use 3 x 5 postcards or 4 x 6 postcards. My answer is that you should use what you think will bring in a buyer very quickly. I prefer oversized four-color postcards because they are inexpensive to mail and very eye-catching. Unlike flyers, you can send postcards through the mail. You could either send them as bulk mail, or you could use USPS.com to send them out for you.

Before you send postcards out, you need to know whom you want to send them to (i.e., your target audience). Not only that, you need to know where you are going to mail them; is it to zip codes, individual cities, or streets? You should know your targeted area. This is why it is vital for you to have a buyers list. If you do not know how to create a buyers list, then you must buy it from list brokers. Before you approach a list broker, you need to give the broker the criteria of what you're looking for, so that the amount you spend acquiring the list will not be a waste.

DIRECT MAILING

Direct mailing is also another viable way of marketing your house. Just like postcards, you need a list of people to send direct mail to. What has worked for me in the past is what is known as a *yellow letter*. This is where I handwrite the letters and send them out. I blanket the area where the house is being sold, with a lot of yellow letters. I also send out letters to the list that I have created and/or purchased from list brokers. I find this also to be a valuable marketing tool.

If an agent represents you, ask him or her about their direct mail program. If the answer is, "We do not have one," then you may want to find out the type of marketing program that is used by your agent. However, whatever marketing that is used, be sure that it yields fast results.

Here are three places to send your direct mail:

1. Neighbors. Everybody has friends and relatives who might want to move near them.
2. Agents who represent buyers in your neighborhood.
3. Buyers who live in other areas but relocate to your neighborhood.

SOCIAL MEDIA

Social media is sweeping the nation like wildfire. If you do not know how to use social media, you may want to hire somebody who knows how to use Facebook, Snapchat, Twitter, or LinkedIn, to advertise your properties for you. By using social media, I have had much success in selling and renting many houses. One of the important things about social media is that it is not confined to people in this country alone. Anyone, in any other country, who is trying to migrate to the shores of the

United States, can see your house and start negotiating on it before they get here.

OPEN HOUSES

Not every house is suitable for an *open house*, due to the location or other factors. Sometimes the only way to determine if having an open house would work for you is to try it. If nobody shows up at your open houses, that is probably a good indication that the strategy may not work for you.

However, if your house is located near a high traffic area, where buyers often swarm through your house to take a look at it whenever you have an open house, then that should be good news for you. It tells me that your house is a good candidate and would be sold in no time.

Once you decide to have an open house:

- Place an Open House sign in front of the house.
- Place the duration of time that you will have the open house.
- Place directional signs on the streets throughout the area to direct the potential buyers to the house.
- Advertise your open house in the newspaper.
- Advertise your open house online.
- Invite the neighbors to your open house, since they are going to come anyway.

Below are SOME pointers that you may want to consider seriously as you market your property with the intention to sell very fast. More than likely, if your house stays on the market for an extended period without selling, it may be because of the poor quality of your marketing efforts. So, what is it that constitutes good marketing, and what is it that constitutes lousy marketing? Let us explore below:

GOOD MARKETING TIPS

- Look for the things that make your house unique, and highlight them in your marketing brochures.
- Ask yourself as to what motivated you, the investor, in the first place, to buy, fix, and then sell it. Once you answer this vital question, be sure to amplify those factors in your marketing materials. This will positively motivate your potential buyer.
- One of the things that I hardly see during open houses these days, is creativity. Should you decide to have an open house, I would advise you to cater in lunch for your clients. Do not be stingy. Try as much as possible to go beyond the little sandwiches and bottled water. Remember, food can be inspiring. Be creative, and count it as an investment. Do not let anybody kid you about this. It will go a very long way — especially when you advertise that food will be served; people will show up.
- Making your open houses entertaining can be rewarding. Try to offer small gift certificates by offering drawings.

Best Ways to Market and Sell Your Properties (Part 2)

- If at all possible, offer your buyers some amount of money or credit toward closing costs. This generous offer would entice anyone to choose your house above others.
- Another thing that you may want to advertise is a *home protection plan*. This could be a deal maker. Once your buyer finds out that potential repairs to the house have been paid for, for at least a year, they would jump and buy your house.
- In a community where there are homeowner association fees, it would look great if you could prepay it for your buyer, for at least a year.
- How about bait for a weekend getaway for two?
- Against all popular belief, place your advertisement in the Sunday classifieds, as well as in the daily newspapers.
- Do not put your ads without pictures. Be sure that the photographs have high resolution to enable your potential buyers to print them, should they decide to do so.

AVOID BAD MARKETING

Publishing Bad Photos

One thing that you should know is that pictures speak volumes and are easily noticed, before any description or words about your home. If the first thing that a potential buyer will see is the pictures that you place online, why not leave a perfect impression rather than a wrong first impression? Remember, first impressions are always lasting impressions.

The real reason why you need pictures of your house is to convert the curious buyer into an actual buyer. Placing poorly shot photos would give the potential buyer a flimsy excuse not to buy your home instead of jumping on it with excitement.

Withholding Important Information or Descriptive Comments

This could be disastrous, especially when the market is saturated with tons of homes. Merely placing a property address, and the number of bedrooms and baths, is insufficient information for a home buyer. It doesn't tell him or her why he or she should make an appointment to see the home, let alone place an offer on it.

Good marketing tells a buyer why your home is better than the dozens of others on the market. Mention the improvements that you have made to the house: the additions that you created; the new flooring, windows, doors; the bathroom additions, with elegant, modern-style faucets; the updated kitchen, with new cabinets; etc. Focus on items like these, and you will be sure to sell your house in no time.

Underestimating the Importance of Broker/Agent Previews

Just like buyers, agents don't have the time to look at every home on the market. The question then is, what can you do to entice them to see your house and bring in buyers? Because agents are more likely to sell a home they have toured, you need to do whatever it takes to attract selling agents.

Best Ways to Market and Sell Your Properties (Part 2)

Restricting Access for Showings

If an agent can't easily show your house, he or she will take their clients somewhere else. She would instead show another person's listing that is easily accessible. Don't give a realtor any reason to pass over your house.

Any of these can hamper showings:

- Where there is no lockbox anywhere on the property.
- Where you have restricted hours to show your house.
- Where you always need 24-hour notice before your house could be seen.
- Where the showing is by appointment only.

Offering Less Commission than Other Listings

Whether an agent has your complete listing or not, know that their income is solely based on commission from sales. Although it is not a bad thing to negotiate the commission if it is too high (e.g., 7%–9%), do not try to beat the agent all the way down until they become so disgruntled that they don't want to show your house, let alone list it.

Whenever the commission that you are willing to pay is very low, agents will view your lower-commissioned listing as the investor/seller that is not motivated to sell. To the agent, you are a time waster.

- If a real estate investor is not motivated to sell, that is a flag that you will not negotiate on price or agree to concessions down the line.
- Whenever the market slows down and turns to a buyer's market, agents and buyers will expect to negotiate. If you are unbendable, your house will stay on the market for a long time.
- If a buyer is asking his or her agent to negotiate with you, but realizes that you are inflexible, then agents will not be enthusiastic about showing your house. Agents would rather show listings where negotiations will be possible, should the buyer demand it.

Not Including Buyer Incentives

As mentioned above, you, the investor/seller, must be willing to offer some incentives that could entice your potential buyer to convert quickly. I am not asking you to offer a Tesla or a helicopter. The stimulus does not have to be excessively expensive. The incentive should not have to cost you an arm and a leg. Be reasonable and make it very attractive. A lovely plant, flower, or grocery gift card are just a few examples that would be appreciated.

Keeping the Price of Your House a Secret

If you are selling your house, then let the population know that your home is for sale. Publish the price so everyone in the neighborhood will know. Do not keep it a secret, unless you are just testing the market to see if it would eventually sell. If you are serious about selling, then it would be suicidal to keep the price hidden.

I wish you the best of luck as you implement these strategies to market and sell your house VERY QUICKLY!

Go for it BIG!

Chapter 11

Get a Power Team Together

"Teamwork makes the dream work, but a vision becomes a nightmare when the leader has a big dream and a bad team."
– John C. Maxwell

To succeed as a real estate investor, it is imperative for you to look for a group of professionals whom you can depend on to help you to achieve your goal and realize your dreams. These individuals are known as a Power Team. When you take your time to search for them, and articulate clearly what it is that you want them to assist you with, they can help you tremendously, and also serve you well to arrive at your destination— From Point A to Point B.

You may ask the question: "Why should I put a Power Team together?" My answer: If you want to operate your business as a true business, and if your goal is to succeed and create wealth, you need people who are experts in areas that you are not good at, to handle the day-to-day activities that you have no time, nor the expertise, to accomplish.

The work of the real estate investor involves quite a bit. From making offers to inspecting properties, locating properties, rehabbing properties, listing properties when ready, meeting with tenants, and performing a host of other tasks that you have no experience in, is just too much work for one person with a determined goal to become wealthy.

Some of my fellow investors, if not most of them, like to perform tasks that they have no business doing in the first place. There are many things that you, as a real estate investor, must consider abstaining from. As I suggested earlier, before you decide to take on any task, you must ask yourself some vital questions: "Is my time worth $10 per hour to accomplish this kind of task? Is my time worth $15.00 per hour to perform this kind of work?" If your answer is an emphatic No, then you need to delegate whatever task you are trying to do without any expertise, to someone else, to execute on your behalf.

Spend your precious time on something that would add more value to your company and more value to the marketplace. Stop cleaning toilets yourself. Stop mowing lawns yourself. Stop doing repairs yourself. Even though, to you, the task at hand may seem so small and trivial, and even though you may think that you could complete it in a short amount of time, on most occasions, you will find yourself spending and wasting a lot of your valued time that you could have devoted to something more beneficial. Hire someone else to do the work for you. We call this Other People's Time (OPT). On any given day, when you have something to be done that could be delegated, ask yourself the question, "Who is going to do this?" Trust me when I say that you will find the appropriate person to accomplish the assignment for you.

The task of finding and putting the right people on your team can be daunting. It is therefore essential that you take your time to find the right people. You will blame yourself if you don't choose wisely. With the right people in place, you would realize that accomplishing your goal would be much easier, faster and quicker. It would make a massive difference between a lucrative profession and someone who is just shooting darts in the dark, without knowing where he or she is headed.

Treat this topic as one of your top priorities as you get on the road to real estate wealth. It is worth repeating that the people that you place on your team must be professionals and experts. Do not hire someone just because you feel sorry for that person, or just because that individual is your favorite relative. Such a mindset will not help but hurt you immensely.

Just think about this:

1. Will a hospital hire you as a medical doctor just because they feel sorry for you?

2. How about this? Let's say that you are a family member or a distant relative of the CEO of a hospital. Will your relative hire you to perform surgery on a patient just because of your status as a family member?

a. Answer: NO

b. Why: Because you have not been trained as a medical doctor. To become a medical doctor, you must go to college and complete the requirements for a Bachelor of Science degree. Then you must pass the MCAT and go to a medical school, and complete the requirements for a medical doctor. Then you must undergo training known as residency. Depending on your choice of specialization, the residency could last anywhere from three to seven years.

c. Since you probably did not go through the rigorous training, or obtain the required education, and since medicine is not your profession, you will cause much havoc and risk the lives of many patients should you be hired to perform the work of a physician.

No one in their right mind would hire you just because you are a relative, or just because they feel sorry for you.

So, whenever you are putting your team together, make sure that you are careful with your choices. Only select those who are well qualified and can add value to your company, and can produce positive results for you.

Let us explore the kind of people or professionals that you will need on your team:

REAL ESTATE AGENT

As a real estate investor, one of the team members that you will need is a realtor or a real estate agent. Whenever you are looking for a realtor to place on your team, look for someone with an outstanding reputation, and one that knows real estate investing. Such a person must also possess knowledge about the area(s) that you would like to invest in.

The agent must understand what you do, what you are looking for, your choice of properties, and the formula that you use to present offers, and they must have the desire and willingness to work with you. Sometimes it is very difficult for real estate agents to understand investors, especially when it comes to making and presenting offers on deals that you, the investor, may deem lucrative.

From my personal experience, real estate agents do not typically want to submit lowball offers. They would instead present higher bids on properties that would fetch them more commissions, rather than create a deal that would make sense for you, the investor. I used to have a very high turnover of realtors, until I found one that understood what I needed and valued the mission and vision of my company. Before then, real estate agents would dictate to me what my formula should be, what my buying criteria should entail, and what offers (high) to present on deals.

This is why it is crucial that you must know exactly what you want. Once you know what it is that you are looking for, then you can intelligently articulate and communicate with real estate agents, and convince him or her to join your team. If and when you find a good agent, one that is eager to make your dreams come true, I would suggest that you pay them more commission than what their counterparts receive from other investors.

Be true to your words. The spoken word is nothing to be taken lightly. Once you make a promise, make sure that you stick to it. If no one trusts you, then guess what? It would be difficult to have people work with and for you. Whenever the realtor realizes that you keep your word, thereby establishing trust, he or she will do your biddings without thinking twice about it.

As already mentioned, one of the advantages of having a realtor on your team is because agents have access to the Multiple Listing System. The agent will also provide you with a significant amount of information on how the market is doing, in regard to listed and sold properties in your target area(s).

Again, it is good to be upfront with the agent about your intentions as an investor. Do not leave them guessing. It is a dangerous practice!

APPRAISER

Another vital individual that you need on your team is an appraiser. An appraiser is an individual that would assess the value of a property and tell you what it's worth. Acquiring properties is not an easy task especially if you don't know what you are doing. As mentioned on numerous instances, you need to know the after-repair value of a property before you make an offer on it.

An appraiser can tell you what you could sell the property for once it is fixed. If you are fortunate to have a very good appraiser, who is also experienced, that would be a plus for you. Such qualities will add tremendous value to your team. So, as you look for an appraiser to join your team, remember to look for one that is well versed in your targeted areas. Also, you need to get someone who can guide and advise you as to what you need to do when you hit a roadblock, and are not able to quickly decide if you should go forward to pursue a deal, which you may deem profitable, or walk away from it.

You may ask why these qualities are necessary in an appraiser. Now, let me tell you. During 2007 and 2008, before the real estate bubble, several appraisers were going around inflating the values of properties. All you had to do was to tell an appraiser what number you wanted a particular deal to reflect, and they did it for you. If you wanted a house to appraise for $200,000, the appraiser made sure that such a request was honored. This in itself, I believe, contributed immensely to the collapse of the real estate market. So, it is essential, if you are going to have an appraiser on your team, to look for one that is good, one that is experienced, one that is licensed, one that is professional, one that is ethical, and one that would add value to your company.

The reason why I keep stressing the fact that you need an experienced and professional appraiser is that they keep abreast with the market, and can tell you about your targeted areas of interest. What I like about my appraiser is the fact that he tells me, every time, without fail, the good, the bad, and the flaws of a property that I may be considering purchasing. Secondly, he has never failed to give me good ideas regarding the repairs a particular property may need to generate my target net profit.

CONTRACTOR

Having a respectable and an ethical contractor on your team is a must. As a matter of fact, having a couple of contractors on your team will go a long way. Better yet, having back up contractors on your team will help you to hit the jackpot almost every time.

There are people who call themselves contractors but are not. Instead, those individuals are what we call CON MEN. If you are not fortunate or careful, you may end up spending more money on repairs than you anticipated, should you end up with one of those con men on your team.

So, the legitimate question to ask is: "Where do I find principled and decent contractors that will do the work that they are hired to do professionally?"

In my case, I look for them like pearls in the sand. One of the ways that I find good contractors is through referrals from my real estate agent(s). The reason is that realtors come across many contractors or handymen that they have developed relationships with over a period of time. Because of that, they can recommend contractors to people who want to sell their houses but need some repairs or upgrades done to their house before placing them on the market.

Since they work with a pool of contractors, they know who the good ones are to recommend. I count myself fortunate in that I have good contractors that have been referred to me by real estate agents.

Another way that I can place a good contractor on my team is through recommendations from the Real Estate Investment Association (REIA), which I am a member of. REIA is an association for real estate investors. Some of my colleagues on the association are rehabbers. What this means is that they buy properties that need work, they repair them, and then place them on the market for sale. Because of the kind of work that the rehabbers do, you can only imagine the number of contractors that they work with. This is why it is so difficult for some rehabbers to give up or recommend good contractors to other investors. Once they come across the good ones, they keep them for themselves.

Because time is of the essence, most of the investors that I work with do not fool around with contractors that are not serious, or are con men. As such, I do not take for granted any contractor that comes recommended to me by other fellow investors, to place on my team.

Besides the above referrals and recommendations, other sources to consider are home improvement stores, such as Lowes, Home Depot, etc. If everything else fails, and I get desperate, I go to a home improvement store early in the morning to find contractors at the check-out line, and I begin a dialogue with them.

Once I have tested and tried a particular contractor, I place him or her on my team. To test who joins my Power Team, there are specific qualifications that I look for:

Is the contractor licensed and insured? If yes, I ask for copies of his or her:

a. Contractor's license
b. Contractor's bond
c. Workmen's compensation insurance

The license has to be valid and not suspended. I make copies of the above documents, and verify them to be in regular standing. I then follow up to be sure it is still valid and not suspended. Also, I make sure that the contractor does not have complaints filed against him or her through the Better Business Bureau. Lastly, if the contractor does not have workmen's compensation insurance, I do not hire him, since this particular insurance protects me, the investor, and guarantees the job will be completed, and that all materials and labor are paid for.

Get a Power Team Together

If the contractor is terrible, he or she will get angry as to why you are not giving them your credit card to purchase items themselves. They will try to convince you that you do not have the time to waste looking for materials. They would do whatever they can to make sure that they purchase materials without you being present.

I remember when this guy on my team told me about a broken air-conditioning unit in one of my rentals. I must admit that I was very suspicious in that the air-conditioning unit was not bad. If anything at all, it needed recharging. I don't remember what he did but he came up with a long list of parts that needed to be purchased before he could repair the air-conditioning for my tenant. I then asked where he was going to buy the parts. As soon as he gave me the address, I decided to meet him there to purchase the parts and pay for them without giving him my credit card number.

He became outraged and started yelling and calling me names when I showed up just because I refused to give him my credit card number. He said I did not trust him and that he would not work with me any longer. Although he claimed to have repaired the air-conditioner, I ended up replacing the air-conditioning unit completely. So, be cautious when it comes to contractors. Look for a professional that would finish the job.

Also, do your best to create time to inspect the job when completed, before you pay the contractor. You will only have yourself to blame if you do not inspect the work. I would normally pay my contractors on draws. All of this is placed in the contract and signed by my contractors.

Once you find that contractor to place on your team, he would, in turn, find a rehab crew that he would work with. That would free you from wasting time and looking for people to work on your properties.

It's worth reiterating:

1. The one who joins your team should be qualified and licensed, and has you and your company at heart.
2. Be very careful, and be selective to make sure that you get the right person.
3. If you are having difficulties finding an outstanding contractor, go onto Craigslist.com, although it is not always the best thing to do; or you can join Angie's List to find professionals.
4. Contact your local REIA for referrals and guidance.
5. Remember that when you have an excellent contractor, you can delegate estimating your repairs to him. Do not waste time trying to figure everything out on your own. *Time is money.*

ACCOUNTANT

The real estate business deals with lots of paperwork. This includes keeping up with the inflow and the outflow of cash. It behooves a real estate investor to think very seriously of hiring an accountant, or at least a bookkeeper, who can keep up with the bills, the bank statements, and the monthly, quarterly, and annual statements, as well as other various obligations.

My suggestion is that you have a separate bank account for your business. Your business account should be different from your personal bank account. Having a bookkeeper or an accountant would save you time, and many headaches, in the long run. You would be able to keep accurate financial records and statements, and also have a good record of your cash flow. Tax time would not be miserable for you when you have someone keeping your books rather than yourself.

INSURANCE AGENT

As you purchase more properties, one of the things that you have to be aware of is the fact that your properties have to be insured. Having an excellent insurance agent on your Power Team will not only help you a great deal but help you to choose the best insurance option out there, and save you quite a bit of money.

It is worth mentioning that not all insurance agents will insure rental properties or vacant properties. Before you settle on one person, be sure that you ask the hard questions. They must know the type of coverage that you need, how many properties can be covered under a particular policy, and the details of what is covered and what is not covered.

They must also know the difference between a standard property insurance policy, which covers homeowners living on the property, versus a landlord insurance policy, which covers rental properties. Is the agent aware that if a claim is filed on a rental property, but the policy is NOT listed under landlord insurance, the claim could be denied? All these are vital and important questions, which the insurance agent that you place on your team must know.

You, the investor, should also familiarize yourself with the coverage. If I did not take it upon myself to learn the difference in policies before placing an insurance agent on my team, I would not have received rental income from my insurance company when my house got flooded (We had to tear out everything from the home, including the drywall, and rebuild the house from scratch.). Because I went through the policy and determined that the policy did not have the provision of Loss of Rent coverage, I was able to get my insurance agent to add it to all my properties. This is the type of policy that enables you, the investor, to collect the rental amount for the property, for a certain period of time, should you not be able collect it due to a catastrophic incident that may have happened to your property. With an agent on your team, and with the right insurance policy, you will not lose money unnecessarily, which would be impossible to recoup.

MORTGAGE BROKER

Having a mortgage broker on your team is a plus, and would help you to stay ahead of the game. After the real estate collapse, lending money to investors and rehabbers has become very difficult. A mortgage broker in today's lending market would prove valuable to you, since good brokers would keep up with the lending laws and thereby give you excellent counseling. Be sure that you do not waste too much time with one mortgage broker, should you realize that he or she is just wasting your time.

PRIVATE-MONEY LENDERS

Most of my properties were funded with private money. It made it easier for me to purchase properties, rehab them, and list or rent them in a speedy manner, and then pay back the borrowed money with interest as soon as the property sold.

Depending on banks to fund your properties will not only delay you but sometimes cause you to lose profitable deals. Also, guess what? After fooling with banks, and after wasting your valuable time, chances are that they may not fund the property for you despite your hard work of putting the requested documents together. This is why it is essential that you look for individuals with money who are always ready to give you the money to buy the property whenever you need it.

Look for private money lenders, and place them on your team. You need to be always looking for such individuals. You would be amazed how you can do several deals, while investors with little cash would be struggling to raise funds to close on properties. The more money you have to disburse to fund your properties, the better. Do not be shy about this at all. Just as oxygen is good for the body, so is readily available money good for the real estate business.

ATTORNEY

In today's world, I will contend that it is not only crucial but critical for you to have a reputable attorney on your team. The world has become unpredictable and dangerous. Without an attorney to set up your corporations, and to craft and look over your paperwork, to be sure that you are well protected, you would be shooting yourself in the foot. From tenants that would not pay rent to buyers who want to sue you for no apparent reason—you need an attorney on your side.

ABOUT THE AUTHOR

Benjamin Oyortey is a well accomplished, savvy, and serial entrepreneur who worked very hard in a coveted finance position, in Corporate America, for several years. He holds an MBA, with concentration in finance, from a prestigious graduate school of business, and a Bachelor of Arts degree in accounting, from Oakwood University.

Benjamin has committed his life to assist humanity. He has done this successfully over the years by changing, mentoring, directing, and improving the lives of individuals who want to attain success but do not have the means or the direction to achieve their goals in life.

Despite his accomplishments, Benjamin was not satisfied. He had this innate drive to be instrumental in the lives of others who were seeking answers to their purpose here on earth. It was with this passion—which motivated him to find a better way for himself, to improve upon his achievements, and to create wealth—that he decided to quit his high paying job and start investing in real estate.

For several years, he has successfully invested in real estate, and has been able to assist individuals, who never thought they could own their own homes, to become proud homeowners. Not only that, he has been very effective in assisting realtors, brokers, and other real estate entrepreneurs to move their businesses to the next level.

Today, Benjamin is a successful entrepreneur in his own right. He is not just an entrepreneur, but he is also an author and a successful investor in diverse businesses. Through these accomplishments, Benjamin has successfully taught others the secret of his success, and as a result, has transformed and continues to challenge others to realize their full potential.